Praise for *The First Advent in Palestine: Reversals, Resistance, and the Ongoing Complexity of Hope*

"Kelley Nikondeha eloquently weaves together the first advent story and the present-day stories of Palestinians, creating invigorating insights for present-day Christians. Palestine then and now, its people, and the politics of the land are a common thread throughout the book, bringing us to a place to genuinely grapple with the meanings of deliverance, peace, justice, and hope. Through her personal encounters, Kelley makes the Palestinian experience visible in a world that has made them invisible. If you are looking for an Advent read that dives into new and raw paths, then *The First Advent in Palestine* is for you."

—Shadia Qubti, Palestinian Christian peacemaker and co-producer of *Women Behind the Wall* podcast

"If you are wearied by or bored with the sentimentality and careless religious nostalgia of American Advent and Christmas, this is the book for you. Kelley Nikondeha takes a deep, alert dive into the natal poetry of the Gospels that has become for us too trite and jaded in its familiarity. She reads this poetry differently because she has, at the same time, made a deep investment in the contemporary life of real people in the actual circumstances of Nazareth, Bethlehem, and Jerusalem, people who happen to be Palestinians who continue to be outsiders to imperial power. The outcome of her bold reading is to see that these Gospel texts initiated a peace movement into the world that defies and subverts the phony peace of every imperialism. This rich, suggestive book permits us to reappropriate in knowing ways the good news of Advent-Christmas, news that destabilizes and emancipates."

—Walter Brueggemann, Columbia Theological Seminary

"A masterful and contextual reading of the biblical story, of suffering and a hard-born hope. Kelley Nikondeha leads readers into a journey through the tiers of multiple oppressions in Palestine from the first advent under the Roman Empire to the current oppression of the indigenous Palestinians under Israeli occupation, highlighting advent as a subversion of imperial power. As a female liberation theologian living in the global south, the author weaves contemporary reality and scripture together, thus uncovering hidden histories and silenced stories, giving a face and a name to the oppressed people, and creating fresh insights into their resilience and faith. A great resource for individuals and churches struggling with the complexities of justice and hope, and a powerful call in the practice of solidarity with the oppressed of this world."

—Mitri Raheb, founder and president of Dar al-Kalima University College of Arts and Culture in Bethlehem

"Beautifully written, Kelley Nikondeha's *The First Advent in Palestine* is empathetic and deeply moving—a call to love both Jewish and Palestinian people of the Holy Land. Reminding readers that acknowledging the real and profound struggles of one people group does not negate the reality and experiences of oppression in the story of the other. Highlighting the often-unknown stories of Palestinian Christians, *First Advent* is a call for liberation and light."

—Rev. Dr. Mae Elise Cannon, executive director of Churches for Middle East Peace (CMEP) and author of *A Land Full of God: Christian Perspectives on the Holy Land*

"Kelley Nikondeha writes with the textual insight of Walter Brueggemann, the historical understanding of Borg and Crossan, and the prose-poetry writing style of Barbara Brown Taylor. She brings her own unique perspective as a Christian with a mixture of Catholic, Evangelical, US, African, and post-colonial experiences. The result is a reading of the advent stories that will illuminate the Middle Eastern world of Mary, Joseph, and Jesus—and our world today as well, so full of agony, anxiety, and pregnancy."

—Brian McLaren, author of *Faith After Doubt* (St. Martin's, January 2021), among many others

After *On the Incarnation* by Athanasius, *The First Advent in Palestine* by Kelley Nikondeha is the best book I've read on the incarnation, peace, and hope. Buy it, read it, and embody it in your community!

—Peter Heltzel, author of *Resurrection City: A Theology of Improvisation*

"Kelley Nikondeha is a modern-day storyteller, and I trust her to speak the truth, even when it's hard. In this book, she thoughtfully and powerfully leans into the gravity of Advent, reminding us that even the best-known stories are complex ones—that's what makes them so powerful. Kelley's words remind us that when the world is hurting, we lean in. We've needed this book for a long time."

—Kaitlin Curtice, author of *Native: Identity, Belonging, and Rediscovering God*

"In a world of protests and splintering religious ideologies, a world longing for peace but preparing for violence, Kelley Nikondeha infuses the often predictable Advent narrative with a sense of place and history that demands engagement. Through scholarship and imaginative theology, and by listening to the current cries for liberation in our world, Nikondeha has written a book that is a love letter to Palestine and the people formed there. It is vital reading, and if you let it, it will change the way you read the story of Jesus's birth—and how you live in light of this transformative event."

—D. L. Mayfield, author of *The Myth of the American Dream* and *Unruly Saint: Dorothy Day's Radical Vision and Its Challenge for Our Times*

"Like so many Westerners, Kelley Nikondeha experienced Advent brightly—angels, shepherds, a star, then a cozy manger scene. Then, her closer look at the Gospel's' advent narratives, framed by trips to Palestine, her life in eastern Africa, and her discovery of the central drama of what has been dismissed too easily as the "intertestamental period," led her to see brutal empire, economic exploitation and hardship, dirty politics, the suppression of women, and persecution. She does not leave us there, though. It is precisely against this darkness that the light of the Savior that she knew all along shines all the more brightly—and calls us to be a light of peace in our darkness today. Every Christian should read this book every Advent—or at any time of year."

—Danial Philpott, professor of political science,
University of Notre Dame

"Advent is often a time filled with attempts to be holly and jolly, making cookies and shopping. With this book, Kelley Nikondeha rescues the season from the saccharine and oversimplified to give us hope—a hope that absolutely has to do with our present day, challenging us to engage in the slow and beautiful process the incarnation set in motion: the disarming practice of restorative justice, peace, and compassion. The author deftly weaves enlightening historical material concerning the political and economic landscape Jesus was born into with moving and beautifully written accounts of her own contemporary experiences among fascinating characters in the Holy Land and beyond. It is a pleasure to read, a call to attention, and a much needed reimagining of what Advent can be."

— Debbie Blue, author of *Consider the Birds*,
Consider the Women, and *Magnificat*

"Kelley Nikondeha walks us vividly through Scripture, history, and the complexities of today. Advent—with its longing, lament, hope, challenges, and calling—comes more alive page by beautifully written page. This book has made Advent more meaningful for me, and I highly recommend it because I believe it will do the same for you."

—Kent Annan, co-director, Humanitarian Disaster Institute
(at Wheaton College)

"The advent story is a story we all relate to, especially Palestinian Christians. During Advent, our Palestinian people connect with the Holy Family, a family with a new child who is born on the margins of society. This book reflects the author's own journey to see beyond the wall separating two narratives. Kelley Nikondeha provides readers with new insights and the invitation to understand Advent beyond any wall of separation."

—Naim Ateek, cofounder of the Sabeel Ecumenical Liberation Theology Center in Jerusalem

"This powerful and poetic book has enriched my faith and deepened my understanding of the first advent. Kelley Nikondeha gets under the skin of the biblical narrative and breathes new life into it—seeing its drama play out through the lens of contemporary Palestinian reality."
    —James Zogby, founder and president of the Arab American Institute
and author of *Arab Voices*

"Kelley Nikondeha's writing is on fire. She set my heart ablaze, inviting us into the ancient advent story with a newness that made me underline and gasp and shout hallelujahs at the page. Read this if you dare."
    —Idelette McVicker, author of *Recovering Racists* and founder of
SheLoves Media Society

THE FIRST ADVENT IN PALESTINE

THE FIRST ADVENT IN PALESTINE

REVERSALS, RESISTANCE, AND THE ONGOING COMPLEXITY OF HOPE

KELLEY NIKONDEHA

BROADLEAF BOOKS
MINNEAPOLIS

THE FIRST ADVENT IN PALESTINE
Reversals, Resistance, and the Ongoing Complexity of Hope

Cover art: Sliman Mansour
Cover design: Olga Grlic

Print ISBN: 978-1-5064-7479-3
eBook ISBN: 978-1-5064-7480-9

For those who carry an Advent ache,
        You are not alone.

May your discomfort with injustice lead you to lament, prayer, and solidarity with the oppressed of this world.

For the people of Palestine,
        You are not invisible.

May your steadfast presence in the land be a blessing as you resist daily acts of oppression.

May our faithful wrestling lead us to a hard-born hope in the God of peace.

CONTENTS

CONTENTS

CONTENTS

10
Homeland, but Not a Home

Holy Family, Return from Egypt

BEGINNINGS

The advent story gifted to me by my faith tradition was one full of angels, shepherds, and even a shining star against a midnight sky. This story lit my imagination with wonder for many years. Until the brightness of the star began to wane.

As I worked abroad in contexts of deep poverty and witnessed hardship at home, I grew more curious about the hope that star pointed us toward each December. I set out to explore the dark edges of Advent so I could better recognize the contours of hope sketched in the stories my tradition has stewarded all these centuries. It seemed the only way to the star was through the darkness.

I wrestled with the advent narratives Luke and Matthew wrote, the opening words about God coming to earth to begin something new, something lasting. It was an admonition to see the world anew as God entered the fray in solidarity with us—what we call incarnation. I began to reckon with these narratives of both grit and glory, and what they reveal about following Jesus in hard places and troubled times.

Reading and rereading the advent narratives, I met an advent that is not primarily a seasonal message about decked halls or strands of white lights or beloved carols. The first advent was about the arrival of God into a world of woe, and every advent since invites us to grapple with what Jesus's coming means to our fraught landscapes now. Marking time with these advent stories, meditating on them each month of the year, allowed me to see the season of Advent as a perennial invitation for the faithful ones.

This book is about the first advent in Palestine, taking the place, people, and politics of the land seriously. The imperial politics and economics are the backdrop to the Gospel narratives, necessary elements in understanding what the Holy Family, and many since, were up against as they tried to survive in hostile territory.

Some call the land of Palestine the fifth gospel because the land reveals much about the life of Jesus.[1] It is definitely true that our ability to grasp the first advent lies in understanding that gospel as well. The more we see the political and economic landscape and the land itself, then, as part of the narrative, the more relevant the advent story will be to us now.

I grew up with what was called a harmonized advent story, one where Joseph and Mary, shepherds, magi, Gabriel, and choirs of angels all coexisted in a singular narrative scene. But this is not the story we were given in the Gospels. In order to return to the stories presented in the original texts, I have written about advent first from the perspective of Luke, and then from the perspective of

Matthew. This allows us to see what they each uniquely say about the arrival of God's peace on earth. This shows us Luke, who sees Rome and Caesar looming even as he tells the story from Mary's viewpoint, as he offers commentary on the economic realities and moments of celebration. Then we meet Matthew, more fixated on Herod's rule and brutality. And we see how Matthew tells the story from Joseph's view, about a father making decisions under duress by means of a series of dreams. The story Matthew writes is a harder advent story, refusing to shy away from the complex dynamics of empire that weighed on the Holy Family. In taking this approach, I seek to remain faithful to both Gospel writers and both narratives. And returning to the Gospel narratives in this way also cracks open fresh conversation about the first advent, and about how we understand Advent now.

Tilling the soil of these advent stories for months on end, I have discovered unexpected things in the dark loam. I was surprised by the trauma that dominated the first advent—how I'd never seen it before, though the tells were all in full view for the astute student of scripture. Factoring in the depth of human distress that surrounds these stories helped me see Zechariah, Mary, and Joseph more clearly. Their struggles became more real. Watching young Mary navigate the tumultuous Galilee region shocked me. For the first time, I entertained a reading of the text that took her resistance, her resolve, and the possibility that she had been abused into account. Her strength has never shone brighter as a result; her song has never sounded more hopeful. And then there emerged the reality of the hard economic life most people endured in Nazareth, Bethlehem, and many villages in between. Concerns about daily bread—and crushing debt, and land loss, and dispossession—saturated the first advent. Advent happened as most people were just trying to survive. The echoes sounded so familiar to my modern ears. I met an advent recognizable to us today as we continue to suffer hardship and hunger for deliverance from troubles personal and systemic, political and economic.

I hope this exploration of Advent will invite you into a similar season of discovery. I hope you won't back away from the hard parts of the story, the uneasy questions the scripture presents, or let it deflate your wonder at the goodness of God's peace campaign afoot. Instead, I pray that an honest wrestling with these narratives will produce an enduring blessing. I pray that you will see the seeds of reversal planted in the soil of Palestine, where women and shepherds and ordinary priests are harbingers of hope. I pray you will see God working the inversion of imperial systems, subverting Caesar's peace with hospitality, solidarity, and lament. And I pray you will see that advent sets the trajectory for the life of Jesus, that what begins with incarnation will culminate in resurrection.

Let's begin.

1

SILENCE AND SUFFERING

The Maccabees

Israel | 1 and 2 Maccabees, Lamentations

When we turn toward Advent, the name on our lips is Emmanuel, *God with us*. So much in Christian faith relies on what the faithful actually mean when we say that name. Western Christianity has forsaken a deep understanding of Advent for strands of twinkling lights and the anticipation of seasonal pleasures. When we accept sentimental expressions and concede to holiday hurry, we miss the original gravity of Advent. We miss understanding how God's arrival, how *God with us*, shapes our ability to see the breaking in of God into a landscape, a people, a narrative—and what the earthly trajectory of the life of Jesus implied then and implies now.

How God entered the world matters. Where and when God chose to come into the world carries significance. Advent is not about one season of devotion; rather, the advent narratives orient us toward a lifetime of faithfulness to the God of liberation, love, and peace.

The stories told around and about the birth of Jesus set our sights on a deep theology for troubled times, then and now. Advent pays attention to the people, places, and politics of generations awaiting God's arrival.

To approach Advent in its fullness, we approach it from an uncommon entry point: the darkness of suffering, the struggle of a long waiting. Confronting the hard landscapes of the past allows us to understand the terrain God entered one starry night. If God can speak comfort and joy into ancient trauma, then the advent of hope awaits us too in our feral world. Into times of suffering also come words we are given for these times. As the angel says, "Don't be afraid." *God is with us.*

❖ ❖ ❖

The first advent began in darkness and danger. Before light or its warmth came, generations of the Jewish people of Judea suffered at the hands of one empire or another. Each successive generation endured another wave of occupation. More sons lost in battle, more land confiscated, more hopes dashed. First the Greeks, then the Egyptians, then the Seleucids each took their turn. Invaders razed towns. They enslaved women and children. Some crucified the rebels. Advent would come to a traumatized landscape and people—but not quite yet.

In the world that waited for deliverance, between the Old and New Testaments, stood four hundred years of silence. Or at least that's what the church I grew up in told us. God didn't speak. There was no record. Nothing of consequence happened during this time. The church referred to those intertestamental years as The Silent Years. The last thing God said on the record was to the prophet Malachi, a word about the uprooting of evil in the land and God's coming justice. So began the long wait for advent, we were told.

What was left out was the truth of Jewish suffering during those dark centuries. And that suffering is the honest prologue to the first advent. Four hundred years of empire and captivity when there wasn't silence at all.

My mother had a heavy Jerusalem Bible, a relic from her Catholic days. It was thick with books I never even knew existed before: books like Tobit, Judith, and Maccabees. They sat between the two testaments, a clue that something happened in those "silent" years after all. These books relayed the stories of people trying to survive, about battles won and lost, about season upon season of pain suffered by Jewish people through four dark centuries. Finding these books hidden in my mother's Bible cracked open for me the possibility that there was more to be discovered.

It would be years before I returned to the pages of the Apocrypha and began to unlearn the theological trope of the silent years. And years before I could see the Jewish struggle to survive those impossibly difficult centuries that predated advent.

The space in between testaments offers the first truth to be grasped: wrestling with suffering is the predicate to God's deliverance. Jewish struggle fomented advent among ordinary men and women living nearest the bottom of the imperial order. The books of 1 and 2 Maccabees detail the devastation and loss in those years. This time, it was the Seleucid Empire's violence and economic exploitation that cornered the Judeans. More loss, more ache, more darkness ensued. Once again the Jewish people were trapped, a familiar and seemingly endless sensation leading up to the first advent.

❖ ❖ ❖

Central to the stories within the two books of the Maccabees is one family, Mattathias and his five sons. They lived in a small town in the hill country of Judea in the second century BCE. Seleucid soldiers roamed the region like a present darkness, harassing the Jews. As a priest, Mattathias likely got more than his fair share of trouble from the soldiers, who shared their king's disdain for the religion of the Jews. King Antiochus Epiphanes famously rode into Jerusalem, fresh off a victory in Egypt, and entered the temple of the Judeans on his horse, trampling the holy place. A sacred fire called the Everlasting Flame burned there. He dared to snuff it out—that sign of God's continual presence with the Jewish people. He took the golden lampstand as booty.[1]

You could almost hear the priest telling his sons more than once: "He took the light from us."

Soldiers were no longer *out there*, but now they were inside the most intimate and holy place. A priest could scarcely fathom such a grievous violation. What would life for his sons and their sons be without the Everlasting Flame? Everything he had taught them about who they were and how to live in the land began to unravel the day the light went out. "Who are we without God's presence? What will become of us if God forsakes us?" These were the questions of every Jewish father, Mattathias chief among them. Deep disorientation shook the Jewish soul.

The world stopped that day. Weddings were postponed. The young lost their energy for anything other than grief. Rulers and elders, brides and their grooms all traded celebration for mourning.[2] Dirges were the only songs heard across the land. What had happened in the temple was like suffering another death.

❖ ❖ ❖

Maybe Mattathias reached for the book of Lamentations and recited the poems of grief handed down from the Jews before him. They had survived the Babylonian destruction of the first temple in 587 BCE and were acquainted with catastrophic loss. It was another time when the Jewish people were hard-pressed and left without the light of the Everlasting Flame. The ancestors knew what it was like to see Jerusalem bent with dishonor and unable to shine. Mattathias likely found solace in rehearsing the laments of his forebears, comforted by their companionship in his sorrow.

In the book of Lamentations, the destroyed city of Jerusalem is personified as a broken and bereft woman, bent with shame. She cries out, "There is none to comfort."[3] Her lament is loud and insistent. Likewise, 1 Maccabees speaks of the desecrated temple as a dishonored woman. The echo connects readers across moments of collective loss for the Jewish people and invites the natural response to such trauma: lament.

Remember, the loss and lament of Mattathias and his kin happened on the historical eve of the first advent. This is what it looked like in the lead-up to God's arrival—very dark and very loud.

Perhaps Mattathias found more than comfort in the book of Lamentations. Even in the grief of captivity, his ancestors planted seeds of hope: "The steadfast love of the Lord never ceases, his mercies never come to an end; they are new every morning."[4] The darkness is not without light, as lament is not without hope.

Maybe Mattathias fanned the flames of hope too as he waited for deliverance from this miserable empire. But it was destruction, not deliverance, that met his hopes this time.

❖ ❖ ❖

As I studied these ancient books and histories, they grounded my present and gave me a place in the larger arc of enduring narratives. The old stories spoke fresh words about where I stood in a sometimes disorienting landscape. The stories I discovered in my mother's Jerusalem Bible nourished my curiosity, but now they also offered a bridge between canons. I discovered stories that gave shape to what once was mere silence, exchanging emptiness for the exploits of Daniel with a dragon and his rescue of the lovely Susanna from an unjust death, fierce Judith beheading a general to free her people, and the Maccabee family fighting the empire. Mattathias, most of all, became my companion. We stood together across the centuries recognizing the loss wrought by empires, responding with lament as we awaited God's liberating arrival.

The Book of Lamentations, in particular, helped me understand the theological tenor of those intertestamental years as a prelude to the advent narratives. This insight I owe to Mattathias. The lamentations on his lips allowed me to see that grief work is the seedbed for Advent hope. We cannot grasp the fullness of the advent narratives to come without attending to the brokenness of our world. Lament is how we name and honor what has been lost or taken from us by one empire or another.

The intertestamental narratives began to answer lingering questions about the road to Advent. The stories included struggle and lament—tales of woe that felt oddly contemporary. In the company of these ancestors I was not alone. These writings voiced something familiar, yet fragile. Sometimes the Spirit moves through the

most unexpected texts, ones somewhat hidden or over-
looked in our Sunday liturgies. The profound sadness of
the Maccabees and Lamentations prepared me for God's
arrival, tilled the soil of my soul so I could receive good
news in due season.

❖ ❖ ❖

When Antiochus Epiphanes came again to Jerusalem
two years later, he destroyed the city. His soldiers set
Jerusalem ablaze, tore down houses, and demolished the
city's high walls meant to protect the Jewish inhabitants.
Women and children were taken captive. The temple
was desecrated—this time with the sacrifice of pigs on
the altar, utter sacrilege in Jewish tradition. The invaders refortified the city, now building their own walls and
taller towers, turning the city of David into a Seleucid
citadel.[5]

It felt like Babylon all over again. The shame impacted
every Jew, but for Mattathias, who had once served in
the temple, his very heart was pierced. "Why was I born
to see this, the ruin of my people, the ruin of the holy
city . . . ?"[6] he cried, adding to the laments of his ancestors.

The king and his men went from town to town,
forcing the priests to sacrifice to foreign gods. But when
Mattathias was confronted with forced servitude and the
command to offer a sacrifice for his village, he could wait
with hope no longer. Taking hope into his own hands,
he refused to make a sacrifice to any god but YHWH.[7]

He killed the fellow Jew who was willing to do the offering in his place. He killed a government official too. Then Mattathias and his sons fled. They hid in the hills—and plotted rebellion.

Some say Mattathias planned the Maccabean Revolt and participated in the early battles. Some say he joined in the forced circumcisions of other Judeans.[8] Perhaps the desecration of the Holy of Holies drove him to pursue holiness at all costs, using violent means to purge the land and purify the people. Other historical testimony says little is known about Mattathias after his murderous outburst and retreat to the hillside. Maybe he faded away in a spirit of repentance, a lament on his lips. Whatever the story of that silence, he died before seeing the light return to the temple.

Before the first advent, then, Mattathias wrestled with the reality of darkness, accompanied by the texts of lament—and hope. This intertestamental everyman reveals the human struggle against oppression on personal and political levels. This everyman asks with us in troubled times: How do you hold on to hope? Do you keep waiting for relief to come, for the fire to be relit? Or do you try to hasten its arrival?

❖ ❖ ❖

No more waiting, no more hoping, no more lamenting. The five sons of Mattathias began a military campaign against the Seleucid Empire. At first, they suffered punishing military defeats, compounded by the death of their father. But they carried on. They fought the Seleucid army guerrilla-style all the way to Jerusalem. For the Maccabees—a name derived from the third son and lead warrior, Judas, called Maccabeus, "the Hammer"—fighting was the only way back to the Holy City.

Indeed, the Maccabees hammered their way through village after village until they reached Jerusalem—and there they won. It was David defeating Goliath, the small militias overcoming the powerful empire, evicting them at last. For the first time in centuries, the Jewish people experienced liberation from foreign rule. Judea rejoiced.

Then came the work of restoration. The Maccabees entered the temple to reclaim their holy place. Weeds grew everywhere. The altars bore signs of sacrilege and abuse. All the lamps and altar pieces of value had been stripped and stolen. The place where the Everlasting Flame once burned bright was empty.

With each stone removed, a new one was set in place; with each weed plucked, each vessel found, life returned to God's sanctuary. One jar of olive oil was discovered, enough to begin: a priest at last lit the Everlasting Flame. God was with them. The rededication of the temple was complete.

Deliverance. After long seasons of embattlement and loss, liberation comes. We pluck the weeds out and plant new gardens in a spirit of rededication. God's mercy

arrives anew, and we almost forget our merciless enemies who devoured our land and loved ones for centuries. Almost—because what mother can forget her child?
What family can forget their patriarch? What people
can forget their high places and homes? Even as the light
shines in the darkness, lament keeps the record.

But in the wake of the rededication of the temple, the
surviving sons of Mattathias did not inaugurate God's
peace, as many had hoped. The hammers continued a
bloody campaign to convert others to their brand of religious devotion, which included forced circumcisions in
surrounding provinces. During the Maccabees' reign,
power struggles were incessant throughout the region,
including fighting within their own ranks. The pain that
initially pushed them toward violence continued to manifest during their tenure. This was not what God's peace
was meant to look like. So maybe the light shined, but
dimly.

The Maccabean era was short-lived. Soon enough
the Romans came. Once again, the Jewish people were
plunged into decades of darkness, suffering under
another empire. One round of violence did not prevent
the next, and God's peace remained on a distant horizon,
yet to be seen.

❖ ❖ ❖

I came of age during a wave of charismatic fever and conversations about what was then referred to as "the now

and the not-yet kingdom of God."[9] My faith community lived in the tension of a kingdom as both present and future reality. We wrestled to embody the slow-rolling and incomplete reign of God on earth as we anticipated a fullness to come. I had tenure in this tension of now and not yet.

As I sat with Mattathias and his kin, a collection of hammers and hopers, I found myself in this tension again. Only this time I stood in the not-yet, the season when nothing sat on the horizon, according to the naked eye. Even as my tradition told me that light and peace were now on offer because Jesus had arrived, my sensibilities lingered longer in the not-yet of Advent. Too often I felt rushed into joy, rushed into hope. Mired in the hard side of anticipation, I leaned into the not-yet of deliverance, the not-yet of God's peace, the not-yet of a world set right by justice for the most vulnerable ones. Within me, a hunger grew for a present sign of relief, for the now to respond to the not-yet. And the surprise was that the light came from the candles of a menorah, from the Hanukkah tradition of my Jewish neighbors. Their practice of waiting with sustained hope amid the world's worst lit my imagination for God's arrival. Now I saw a small light.

Hanukkah celebrates liberation and light. It commemorates the Maccabean victory against all the imperial odds, and the rededication of the temple. While the triumphs were fleeting, resolve and resilience emerged as hallmarks of the Jewish people, exemplified by the candles of the menorah lit ever since.[10]

In the midst of humanity's worst—ghettos and genocide, anti-Semitism in society, supersessionism in Christian theology, the constant fear of annihilation and the resulting communal trauma—comes Hanukkah within and through all parts of the Jewish catalog of suffering. The suffering is seen and survived. It is named and lamented. But always there is the faintest bit of hope as the remaining oil keeps the fire lit, pushing against the darkness.

One thing you can do in the dark is light a candle. Another is tell a story. In Hanukkah, both happen while we await the arrival of an everlasting peace.

❖   ❖   ❖

Those centuries loud with Jewish suffering, injustice, and lament in 1 and 2 Maccabees were never meant to be silent or invisible. They could have been part of the story I knew, the agony I saw, if I had held on to that Jerusalem Bible with its extra books that told the story. But I was given a different canon of biblical texts, which hid the pain and offered another story—the narrative of a God who was silent for four hundred years.

The reality, the history, matters for our understanding of the first advent and for a more honest reckoning with the fears of our Jewish neighbors.

In each year's celebration of Advent in the Christian tradition, not only was the story of the Maccabees silenced, but no mention was made of the other ancient people of the land—that excision having a modern correlation. Those who lived in the Holy Land alongside the Jewish people were never named, even as Palestinians had equally deep roots in the same sacred soil.

Yet the Christian tradition I grew up in—and many others—perpetuated the silence of Jewish suffering. And the church also silenced the story of other people who called the land home. The Palestinian presence was as invisible as the Jewish suffering during the intertestamental period.

❖ ❖ ❖

In the early 1990s, after hearing so much on the nightly news about the roiling Middle East, including the first Intifada protests against Israeli occupation in the West Bank,[11] I looked for a book that might offer a clear understanding of current issues in the region. I picked up a bestseller at the time, *From Beirut to Jerusalem*,[12] in which I read for the first time about the long history of Palestinian people and Jewish people in the same land. I also learned that some Palestinians embrace the Christian faith, sharing my own tradition. I began to understand that the current issue was also an ancient one, extending further back than even the Egyptian, Seleucid, Greek, and Roman occupations of the region. The book offered me a new frame in which to view my Christian upbringing, including what had been left out of the texts and histories I was given. This prompted an epiphany for me:

nowhere in my Christian tradition was the story of the Palestinian people told. Now I was confronted with the reality of the Palestinians living in the same territory I'd studied in the scriptures my entire life. I saw clearly for the first time a history that had been intentionally hidden. The memory of that realization still stings.

I considered myself a faithful Christian and a faithful reader of the texts in my tradition, and all the while, I never saw the Palestinian people. I never saw Palestinian suffering. But once I did see, I could not look away. This led me to think more deeply about these hidden histories, and about others that have gone untold. I vowed never to forget those four hundred years and the suffering of not one but two peoples with a history in that land.

For nearly thirty years, I have been reading the deeper histories and seeking to live with my eyes and heart wide open to bear witness to the truths I was never told— the suffering of the Jewish people, the suffering of the Palestinian people—and to gain an understanding of the land they hold in common. As I journeyed toward restitution, continually reading, growing in friendships with Palestinian neighbors, and visiting Israel-Palestine, I knew that taking the blinders off was the only option. That, and giving voice to the narratives.

❖ ❖ ❖

As we consider the land that hosts our Advent stories and hopes, we will meet with our own resistance. Leaning into the sorrows of the place will recalibrate our vision and open us to a wider experience of God. Attentive presence to receive Advent's word for troubled landscapes will be what calls us forward.

The Holocaust is among the tragedies we know and name. The resolve to *never forget* has been bolstered by history books, literature, and films that serve as ready reminders of the deep loss Jewish people have suffered in recent decades. We can surely understand how survivors would look toward their historic homeland for safe harbor in this hostile world, even if some people remain uneasy with how the formation of the modern-day nation of Israel was carried out.

But seldom have we listened to the histories and stories of the others in the land—the Palestinian families also rooted there for thousands of years, and then displaced by the creation of the state of Israel. If we see Palestinians at all, it's through the lens of an unforgiving media that portrays them as the terrorists of the region. Invisible to us are the checkpoints, routine home demolitions, restricted access to water, and economies strangled by design. Silenced are the events of 1948 when families were pushed out of homes with only keys in hand, or the Six-Day War of 1967, which took even more ancestral land from Palestinian families, or the Oslo Accords, brokered by the United States in 1993, which failed to deliver a workable peace but rather ensconced yet more division. We have empathized with Jewish pain and understood the nature of their trauma. Yet we have failed to recognize the long land histories, the shared places, where Palestinian families have been traumatized too.

We continue to silence our Semitic neighbors. Israel-Palestine and her people are all saddled with variations on the theme of trauma, a common denominator. From the tumultuous days of empires past to the present uprisings and military actions, the land of Advent still throbs with intense pain. And the ongoing trauma experienced by both Israeli and Palestinian communities makes it hard for each to see the other's humanity and makes violence more likely. A separation wall between the West Bank and Israel finds one side with checkpoints and the other with cement bunkers at bus stops.[13]

Everyone is afraid. Everyone still hungers for liberation and light, for God to arrive again with a lasting peace.

As I have committed to the work of naming suffering—ours and others'—I have also understood that this is the work essential to Advent. Only the pain we name is available for transformation. What I fail to see, I fail to lament. And if I cannot express grief about the brokenness around me, then I remain trapped, a harm to myself, to others.

When we grasp our humanity in all its vulnerability, seeing it unvarnished amid our suffering, the meaning of incarnation penetrates deeper within us. God enters our frail bodies, our hemorrhaging landscapes, and our troubled times. *God is with us* where trauma hits hardest.

That God will rise, scars still etched in skin, should not surprise us, given God's first advent in a land replete with injustice and pain.

For too many people over too many centuries, waiting is not partnered with anticipation. Hope isn't on the horizon. Waiting is a thick sludge of darkness, especially for people made invisible, for people whom empire conquers and traumatizes. To this day, much of the world waits in this way. We are called to see them, to weep with those who weep. It is, after all, a predicate to rejoicing with those who rejoice.

❖ ❖ ❖

For many years now, I have lived with an Advent ache. As the church turned toward the manger and reflected with anticipation on what the coming of Jesus meant in this hallowed season, I stood in a more somber space. Usually alone.

In that somber space, I began making out the shapes in the darkness. What became more visible to me as I leaned toward Bethlehem were those suffering around me—refugees braving dangerous seas to find safety elsewhere, immigrants surviving an undocumented life, families trapped in the Gaza Strip with dwindling potable water. What I saw with stinging focus was an echo of the night before the first advent, the suffering of people near and far.

As cafés and churches were decked with green gar-lands and red ribbon each December, I was learning to see more clearly who inhabited the dark places in our world. I began making out the shapes in the darkness. Not unlike the ancient days, the world I inhabit cries out for lament to acknowledge all the loss.

A vital part of the first advent is wrestling with those harmed by imperial oppressors—from the Babylonians to the Seleucids to the Romans. Advent can include the short-lived victory of the Maccabees, the struggle to sur-vive perilous times and inhospitable terrain. This is the lead-in to the advent narratives.

Advent begins when our Jewish friends light the first candle on the menorah, inviting us into that dark and holy space where we sit in solidarity with others and await relief, maybe even a deliverer, together. And advent carries with it the scars of Palestinians from decades of violence and relinquished hopes in the land.

What does it mean to say *God is with us*? It's harder—and more hopeful—than strands of twinkling lights. When we engage the darkness before God's arrival, we come closer not only to the first advent but also to each one since. In Advent, we learn that God is always coming to our troubled times.

2

GOD'S PEACE CAMPAIGN

Zechariah

Jerusalem | Luke 1:5–25

The ache of injustice and suffering preceded the first advent. So did world peace.

As we connect the dots between antiquity and gospel narrative, this might come as a surprise. But we meet Luke's account, where he reminds readers that the advent story came within a particular time: it all began in the days of Herod.[1] What was left unwritten, but known to Luke's contemporaries, was that Herod ruled under the auspices of Rome. At this point in history, Caesar was in control of the region—and much of the world.

While Rome ruled Judea and the surrounding provinces, a decisive military victory in Egypt ended decades of war in the Mediterranean and united the known world under Rome's banner.[2] Caesar inaugurated the *Pax Romana* (Roman Peace). No one before had accomplished such a feat. And many declared Caesar the savior of the world, the one who ended the cycles of endless war.

So why did God choose this time in human history to enter the world through the vulnerability of incarnation? Why come when peace had finally arrived?

For me, an additional question remained: Was God's advent a divine redundancy? But as I read the histories, I also saw *how* Caesar's peace had arrived: through crushing victory and control maintained through violence against those subject to his rule. What made some see Caesar as a savior was a *kind* of peace that benefited the few while exploiting the many; one that usurped land and harvests from the poor. Perhaps, I thought, the first advent was God's critique of what the world called peace.

Oppression took on different forms, beyond military violence. Those working the fields were required to give over half of the bounty to Rome, leaving little for families to survive on. For those with few means, paying tribute to Caesar, taxes to Herod, and tithes to support the temple created debt, with new systems of bad-faith loans offered by speculators.[3] This world of peace was a world of foreclosures, evicting families from their land, often turning them into tenant farmers on their own property. Economic loss separated families, caused malnutrition in children, and left many women widowed and vulnerable. What looked to a few people of means like a world of peace kept most of the population in a constant position of economic stress by imperial design.[4] Another form of violence.

After world peace was announced by the empire, God began a counter-campaign in the hills of Judea. On offer: a vision of peace with no reliance on violence or war, one that would not turn families out of homes or off their ancestral land. God's peace would be good news to the poor and would cause anxiety for kings and power brokers of the empire. The imperial order would be inverted. Much like jubilee, the economic policy introduced during the days of Moses, this vision for change was good news for families trapped on the underside of a bad economy.[5] And like the jubilee announced centuries earlier, God's peace would come as good news (or hard news—depending on your social position).

If you were a working-class shepherd, a barren woman, a tradesman looking for work, an ordinary priest, or the keeper of a local inn, then good news was coming your way. If you were more like kings and courtiers, those who curried the favor of the rulers and benefited from imperial policies, then the call would come to revisit your loyalties. The advent of God's peace arrived as a grand reversal to challenge expectations about the shape of peace and to bring durable hope to hard times. And God's advent initiative began with an ordinary priest in the hills of Judea, just north of Jerusalem.

❖ ❖ ❖

It was a precarious time to be a priest. Herod played politics with the priesthood, appointing priests from other regions and promoting those who aligned with his interests. He destabilized the expected order to create anxiety for ordinary priests.[6] Every new change to the priesthood functionally demoted priests like Zechariah, who came from a priestly family line, as did his wife, Elizabeth.

Under the increasing economic strain of Caesar's tribute and taxes, people could hardly pay temple tithes. The tithes were collected by the high priests and used to subsidize their opulent lives in the temple precincts of Jerusalem. What little remained went to local priests. During Herod's tenure, Zechariah the priest got ever-lessening support.

Still, good priests in their roles could expect some "blessings" within the social structure created by the Roman-occupied province of Judea. But there was one blessing Zechariah and Elizabeth longed for, one that had never materialized during the many years of their marriage. In a tradition that taught that the righteous would be blessed, these exceedingly righteous ones had no children.

The dissonance is deafening: righteous and barren.[7] The advent narrative of Luke begins here, with a paradox.

In his priestly role, Zechariah served his village most days by teaching the Law, the Prophets, and other sacred writings. He offered counsel and comfort. But week to week, he also needed to find other work to supplement the small stipend he received from the temple.[8] He likely farmed—planting, pruning, harvesting, and even laboring at the threshing floor and oil press in hard years. His aging body probably struggled to work enough to earn enough. A son's help would have been such a blessing in this unforgiving landscape. From Zechariah's vantage point, a chasm existed between the people in his village and the temple elites. Every time he traveled to Jerusalem for his annual week of service, he witnessed the disparity: the ornate clothes, the well-appointed homes inside the city walls, the easy access to power. The priestly elite's ability to see the world aright and to judge with fairness was clouded, even compromised. They were disconnected from the suffering of the people they were meant to serve. A righteous man like Zechariah would have noticed everything.

At the shared meals as Zechariah served his week in the temple, when he saw the elite priests gorge on meat and other delicacies, perhaps he remembered the face of a neighborhood widow who had no food for her children save the loaf of bread Elizabeth shared. Maybe he also held in memory the previous week, when he harvested olives alongside the neighbors, sharing woes in the olive groves about another tax increase, men forced to sell their plots, sons planning to travel north for work in Galilee after the harvest.

The concerns of the temple elites were not the concerns of the village. As he served the high priest a platter piled high with pomegranates, stone fruits, and figs, Zechariah also held the paradox of his neighbors' pain. As an ordinary priest, he stood in a unique position in

Judean society, able to see the economic inequity and to feel its pressure.[9]

Perhaps these paradoxes were the heaviness he carried into the temple as he stood in front of the altar of incense. It was his turn, determined by the casting of lots. Zechariah entered the holy space yoked with barrenness: unfruitful land, sterile futures caused by Caesar's so-called peace, and the absence of future generations in his own priestly line. He carried the ache with him as he went inside to the altar. The first whiff of holy smoke escaped the censer and ascended like a prayer.

❖ ❖ ❖

Each time I visit the Holy Land, I visit with those who even today find it hard to make a living in the neighborhoods of Jerusalem. For centuries, good people like the Razzouk clan have struggled in economically depressed times to serve traveling pilgrims while also supporting their families. The Razzouk family are Coptic Christians who have carried on the tradition of tattooing pilgrims since 1300 CE. The tattoos certify each pilgrim's arrival through the Jaffa Gate in the Old City. The current practitioner carrying on the family work is Wassim Razzouk. He represents the twenty-seventh generation of the family to reside and work in Jerusalem. I've sat with him and his sons for tattoos on those visits to the Holy Land. Each sitting has been sacramental, ink penetrating skin as the ultimate reminder of my journey.[10]

Over a series of visits, Wassim has shared his family story with me. Nearly a millennium ago, they arrived in Jerusalem from Egypt, carrying with them 168 traditional woodcut stamps for the work of tattooing the faithful. An ancestor in the family had learned the sacred art from a Coptic priest.

But relying on tourism and pilgrims made for a precarious living, even in the holiest city. So by necessity, these men (and a few women) were bivocational in order to continue serving pilgrims and support their households. Wassim's family were merchants, running small curio shops and selling various goods in the Old City. His grandfather, Jacoub, made coffins. When the city swelled with pilgrims around Holy Week or Nativity festivities, they tattooed out of the back of their shops or on the steps in front of the Church of the Holy Sepulchre. The economy in Jerusalem remains tenuous for sacramental practitioners.

As I heard Wassim's story in greater detail over the years, I thought the Razzouk clan were not unlike Zechariah, who farmed to serve and survive. And the fact that the Copts, a Christian sect originating in Egypt, were often victims of persecution in the largely Muslim country reminded me of the ongoing struggles for those who hope through dark times. I was told that during the times of persecution in Egypt, the priests would tattoo small crosses on converts' wrists to mark them for entrance into the church, a permanent sign that they were friend, not foe. This was the beginning of the tradition of priests who then trained others in the art of tattooing. Family lore has it that the first member of the Razzouk family to learn the art of tattooing was a priest himself.

❖ ❖ ❖

Down the limestone alley from Razzouk Tattoo are the nondescript courtyard and steps leading into the Church of the Holy Sepulchre, a space marking the traditionally understood location of the death, burial, and resurrection of Jesus. Burnished golden censers hang overhead. The aroma of incense, thick and clinging to those ancient stone walls, reminds visitors of prayers offered across the generations. Sometimes pilgrims can be heard chanting in an upper room as priests burn more incense, adding a fresh layer of petition to the patina. In the sanctuary, you encounter the tangible texture of prayers.

Down the cobblestone streets at the far end of the Old City, I walk to the site of the former temple, where Zechariah once stood. Its walls that long ago likely held a patina of prayers similar to the Holy Sepulchre walls today: centuries of prayers clinging to those temple stones, from priests who came before him.

Luke describes the multitude praying outside the temple "at the time of the incense offering," mirroring Zechariah as he lit the censer inside.[11] There is a sense that the people outside those walls were joined in prayer with

Zechariah inside them, not only in the action but in the content of their petitions. As Zechariah prayed, he did not pray alone. As his voice mingled with the incense, he offered the needs, pains, and hopes of the people.

Maybe as he prayed he saw the faces of workers and widows, the figs that farmers could not afford to eat left half-eaten on the high priest's plate. Maybe he saw sons looking for work in the north, and the downcast fathers who stayed at home. Or perhaps he raised an incense-like prayer recalling the meals he and Elizabeth fasted from to provide for the family next door. "Don't you see us?" you can hear him cry. "How long will we be at the mercy of Rome and Herod and the elites that collude with them? When will the poor have enough to live and the greedy see their pockets empty?"[12]

Facing the altar, Zechariah echoed the people's prayers, the ones he'd heard under the fig tree, the pleas of his neighbors. He carried the reality of their petitions into the holy chamber. He offered communal supplication, shaped by neighbors in the orchards and at the wine press. He prayed their prayers and lamented their losses. A righteous priest, a true friend.

❖ ❖ ❖

He prayed. And as he did, the angel Gabriel appeared and stood beside the altar. The words fell away. Zechariah was frightened. Gabriel spoke into his fears, told him to put them away because he came with good news. Gabriel told

Zechariah God heard his prayer and planned to answer it. He said there would be a son for Zechariah, for Elizabeth. "You will have joy and gladness, and many will rejoice at his birth, for he will be great in the sight of the Lord," the messenger said.[13]

That Gabriel would mention Zechariah's own private pleas uttered as he pulled olives from their branches, as he funneled just-pressed wine into clay jars, and as he walked the uneven road home each day meant that God had listened. When Zechariah blew out the candle at night and whispered his heart into the darkness, God heard. Perhaps God had always been listening to him—and to the cries of the last four hundred years. It meant *God is with us*.

And yet. "How shall I know this?" Zechariah asked, echoing the patriarch Abraham before him. "For I am an old man, and my wife is getting on in years."[14] I wonder if every meeting with something larger than ourselves that speaks to our deepest longings has us responding in doubt. Perhaps all those years of waiting for a son, waiting for a messiah, and awaiting the empire's worst were collectively a trauma to make him—anybody!— slow to believe. For his disbelief, the Gospel of Luke records, Gabriel struck Zechariah mute. Words would wait for the priest until these things came to pass, giving him plenty of time to ponder the what and the why of it all.

❖ ❖ ❖

The people outside were waiting for Zechariah to emerge and complete the ceremony of incense. The priest was taking so long. They continued to wait, the men shifting their weight, letting out sighs, stomachs grumbling. Finally, Zechariah appeared. But he emerged without saying anything. Then as the questions came at him, he offered an awkward pantomime. Most couldn't follow, but a few caught on to his gestures. One might have shouted, "He encountered an angel, like Daniel!"[15] Zechariah would have pointed to him, nodding in wild agreement. A priestly game of charades in the temple courtyard.

Quietly, for there was no other way, Zechariah finished his time of service in the temple. As he headed home, the next frontier awaited—explaining all of this to Elizabeth without words.

But news traveled fast from Jerusalem to the village, ahead of Zechariah's arrival. Before he could make a single sign, she smiled and embraced him. Gladness already encircled the old couple. They were going to have a baby!

Luke reports that in a short time, Elizabeth conceived a child, and that for the first five months of her pregnancy, she stayed out of the public eye. Cloistered in her garden, she savored the joy of the unexpected. She offered gratitude to the God who had remembered her and removed her reproach. Soon enough, the neighbors would see her glory, her body showing the good news.

But for now, the couple waited. In so many previous seasons, they had marked time weighted with heaviness:

Will there be a pregnancy this month? Will there be relief from Herod this time? Will there be a good harvest this season? But this time was different as they waited for a son, waited for Zechariah's words to return so he could announce their good news to the world. Long schooled in patience, this time they waited with joy for the arrival of their baby.

In his months of silence, Zechariah surely recognized how he and Elizabeth followed in the footsteps of Abraham and Sarah: advanced in age and without children, yet visited by God with an astonishing announcement. Did Zechariah consider that, like Abraham's family, his was blessed to be a blessing to others, to his neighbors, to those in the olive groves? Or even beyond?

His prayer for a son was answered in the widest possible way: this son would be a universal blessing as he prepared the way for the Lord to come. Is this what Gabriel had meant about Zechariah's own gladness rippling outward into rejoicing for everyone? Weeping together, but now rejoicing together?

❖ ❖ ❖

Zechariah, a man among the people, lived amid the trauma and tension of his times, and it shaped his prayers.

He prayed from a certain place, for a certain people. His prayers were shaped by life in an occupied land, by economic policies that dispossessed many. His practice of prayer was tethered to his neighborhood, to the friends who lived there.

The incense, the pantomime, the waiting, the embodied prayers of Zechariah began to extend my own experience of Advent prayer. My prayers grew to share a similar tenor connected to land and to neighbors: petitions for refugees in camps in Bethlehem, for people living with little assistance, disdained by elite others who refuse to care. These prayers became prayers for us, for neighbors, for those I walk alongside in this troubled world. Zechariah taught me that if I didn't see my neighbors and their pain, if I refused to join them in solidarity, if I neglected a shared lament, then Advent's first announcement would fall on deaf ears.

❖ ❖ ❖

Expectations in the Judean province were mixed and many, and therefore messy. Some, maybe even Zechariah, expected the return of Elijah the prophet. Others expected a David-like leader to rise from among them to wage a military campaign to oust the Romans. Across the provinces were many messianic movements and a perpetual hunger for relief from occupation. To the naked eye, deliverance wasn't coming anytime soon.

But Luke tells the reader that God is quietly on the move in Judea. The holy seed from the stump that Isaiah once imagined in his arid land would soon emerge—and in Zechariah's own time.[16] Amid an ordinary place and among ordinary people, God had begun a new thing. On the underside of those hit hardest by the economy and by Roman rule, for those poor valued by God, something was clearly on display in this initial advent scene.[17]

The seeds of peace sprout among the meek; their troubled landscape hosts incarnation.

Zechariah, a descendant of generations of Jewish trauma, was an old priest struggling like so many people. Maybe that is why he doubted the angel at first: How could he believe goodness was on offer when for generations God's hand had seemed empty?

When Zechariah left Jerusalem, the resident priests didn't know the content of the angel's announcement. They couldn't decipher an old man's sign language performed with calloused hands stained by the olives of another harvest.

But the story of a couple, of two elders, gave way to a new season, to God birthing transformation in their midst.

The hinge is an ordinary priest standing between the haves and the have-nots, between the empire's beneficiaries and its victims. He interceded in his small village and in the Holy City. The hinge is a barren woman who'd given up on the dream of a child, and then understood that God had reversed her barrenness, creating a whole new peace that would dawn in Judea. This coming peace would not begin on a battlefield, but on a birthing stool.

3
FORMED BY GALILEE

Mary

Nazareth | Luke 1:26–38

With each precursor—the not-so-silent years of the Maccabees, the actual silence of Zechariah that nonetheless told the story of a child coming to prepare the way—the advent scene builds. We have witnessed how God came to an ordinary priest, bypassing the high priest and elites, to begin a new kind of peace campaign. Next, God reached toward Galilee to find a suitable collaborator in the ongoing peace operation. In a culture and a set of stories where priests and patriarchs were given celebrity status, Jewish ears must have burned when they heard Luke's Gospel mention a girl from Galilee.

The advent of Messiah would not look like what any good Jewish man—or woman—expected. And while messianic expectations were varied and messy during the first century, God's rolling revelation seemed to astound everyone in equal measure.

No one anticipated this move—the place or the person God would approach next—least of all the girl in Galilee.

◆ ◆ ◆

Galilee was nothing like its southern sister, Judea. The northern region known for resistance stood ever ready to push back against invading forces, foreign or domestic, and that included the temple-state located in Jerusalem that exacted taxes and tithes from the northern provinces.[1] In a previous season, when the Maccabees defeated the Seleucid Empire, the Galilean villages did not easily welcome their southern siblings.

Even though both Galilee and Judea were among the regions associated with the twelve tribes of Israel, they did not necessarily get along. Judean life to the south centered on the temple and Torah, on Davidic history and hopes. This was not the case with the villages of Galilee. The northern towns hailed from several different tribes and had mixed with other people groups over the course of successive generations of conflict. They were considered lesser Jews because most weren't circumcised and didn't worship regularly in the temple, and because many had intermarried with non-Jewish people. Galileans, according to the Judeans, were simply not the best of people.[2]

Something was always happening in Galilee—altercations, protests, uprisings. The mix of grief and hope manifested in bodies across the agitated landscape. Some turned to armed resistance to defend their homes against foreign forces, others to banditry to cope with economic stress. Periodically, someone who claimed to be Messiah would pop up, galvanizing the aspirations of the disenfranchised population. The incessant push and pull between the imperial militias and local fighters kept everyone on edge. Village life across Galilee was not bucolic and benign, but tense and taut. A toxic mingling of woe, want, and waiting for the next act of aggression created cycles of inescapable trauma for all the inhabitants of Galilee. It was the last place anyone expected to be on God's map for a peace campaign.

❖ ❖ ❖

Once again, God dispatched the angel Gabriel, this time to Galilee; at the same time, new life was unfolding in the womb of a once-barren woman, as if her body was setting the timetable.[3]

Gabriel went to Nazareth, home to some of the branches of Jesse's family tree, from which King David and his sons came, a line that included Ruth—an outsider, an immigrant in a life of loss, poverty, and redemption.[4] There, Gabriel found a virgin betrothed to Joseph, from the house of David, and her name was Mary.[5]

This girl was on no one's list of important people. Growing up in a restive region, she had been formed by resistance. Like most around her, she understood justice as rebellion against empires and their violence. While men in her community took up arms to protect their lives and land, she might have composed songs like her namesake, Miriam of Exodus, did centuries before. Imagine her songs of grand reversals and unlikely victories, songs she sang when the men returned from their forays and the village gathered to debrief the happenings. But she was one girl among many living amid precarious times in a precarious place.

And while she was not yet significant, I doubt she was ever known for being meek or mild.

My travels in the West Bank, a landscape currently riddled with resistance, helped me see what is required of the men and women who call this land home. The hardships of the Israeli occupation—roadblocks, denied construction requests, disrupted water service, incessant harassment from soldiers—can't be ignored. Heavy sighs laden with frustration and angry outbursts are not uncommon. But the people persevere with a ruggedness necessary to endure in their homeland. There is a fierceness that coexists with kindness, a will for survival felt with every shared cup of tea. My times in Bethany, Nablus, and the small village of Kafr Malik outside of Ramallah left me in awe of the daily resilience that resistance requires. Such people are not always genteel, but they are often goodhearted, if direct.

Mary came from Nazareth and was betrothed to Joseph, also a Nazorean. Whether his clan had settled in the village when they returned from exile in Babylon or had migrated from the south during a time of economic duress is a matter of debate. But his family had ancestral roots in Judea.[6] Luke makes clear that Mary is located in the northern town of Nazareth but linked through Joseph's lineage to Judea in the south.[7]

Maybe Nazareth was a Davidic outpost, its people nestled among the Galileans but still loyal to Jerusalem. More likely, the Nazoreans were just like other Galileans after so many generations, speaking with the same accent and suffering the same hardships. In this small, forgettable town, Joseph and Mary began their advent journey.[8]

❖ ❖ ❖

Jewish tradition held that the promised Messiah would come from David's house, though most people looked to the southern town of Bethlehem and to Judea for any signs of hope arising. But over the troubled centuries of empires and exile, of economic hardship and famines, David's descendants had scattered. By the first century, they were found living as far as the northern towns of Galilee. But God never lost sight of the Davidic tendrils reaching into the north, never saw those families as less than their southern kin.

I walked through the ruins of Sepphoris, once considered the ancestral home of Mary. I looked across the shallow valley at Nazareth, thinking of Nathanael's question, "Can anything good come out of Nazareth?"[9]

Nathanael asked this rhetorical question, recounted in the Gospel of John, many years after the unfolding of the advent story. When Philip, a Jesus-follower trying to recruit Nathanael, described Jesus as Joseph's son from Nazareth,[10] he was taken aback; thus the question. Nathanael knew of the small village because he likely hailed from Bethsaida or a nearby town, a short distance from there on the northern shore of the Sea of Galilee. As someone from the same region, he was not belittling Nazareth, contrary to some interpretations. He likely knew good people from Nazareth. But I wondered at his insistence that Messiah would emerge from the south, not a northern village.[11] Was it his lack of imagination, or his adherence to tradition? Indeed, the prevailing thought in Nathanael's day was that the "good," the Messiah, could only come from Bethlehem.

Maybe the story of Nazareth is about exiles' eventual return or about people settling into a new place and starting over after a season elsewhere. Maybe Nazareth is about groups migrating as larger geopolitical realities force them to move against their will. And maybe Nazareth is among the reminders that wherever I move, wherever we move, God goes with us. God shows up there to make good on old promises. As I reread the Nathanael passage now, I am reminded that in unknown and roiling places like the northern village of Nazareth, hopes can still be realized. In unexpected places, good things, even God's kingdom, can come.

In a land divided by north and south, "good" Jew and "lesser" Jew, and all the tribal distinctions, where partisanship was a natural feature of the terrain, God came. Not only for Judeans who had Jerusalem and the temple, who had the land of King David where they expected Messiah would emerge in due season. But God came also to Galilee, which means "circle of the people," a region peppered with villages fighting for survival in a rugged climate never at rest. God came to the entire people.

First, the messenger Gabriel is dispatched to the south, to an ordinary priest serving in the temple, and then to the north, to an ordinary Galilean girl. In Galilee, the angel hints that God is at work in the Judean hills, pointing Mary south to her relative Elizabeth's house. And as the story unfolds, we begin to see that even Joseph straddles regions, living in Nazareth but with filial roots in Judea's soil. There is an evolving sense that God is weaving people together across partisan lines, challenging old animosities and generational rifts to fashion a new kind of peace.

❖ ❖ ❖

A young woman in an unexpected place receives a visit from an angel. She is told that she has found favor with God, despite all evidence to the contrary: her location, her lowly position, even her gender in a patriarchal society. But she's favored, according to the angel. "The Lord is with you," Gabriel insists.[12] Mary is told she will be the locus of incarnation, the place where God enters humanity. The Spirit will overshadow her body, and in her, God will close the gap between human and divine. Her body will begin to accommodate God, to make room before she's even showing.

And, she's told, all this will happen before she consummates her marriage to Joseph.

Three times in the annunciation story Luke tells, the gospel writer makes the point that Mary is a virgin. Did he mean she was literally untouched by any man? Or did he intend to say that she was a young woman without children yet, which is another way to translate the word he used for "virgin"? Was Luke speaking metaphorically, allowing Mary's virginity to contrast with Elizabeth's barrenness?[13]

These are questions the Christian tradition still wrestles with, even as the Holy Land is dotted with shrines and cathedrals in Mary's honor. There might be questions about the nature of her goodness, but we don't doubt that she was good and, as Gabriel said, "favored."

History has continued to wonder about Mary. Some have wondered if she fell victim to sexual abuse: a young girl in a turbulent landscape, where imperial soldiers raped women as part of an ongoing campaign of humiliation and control. As a girl on the verge of womanhood living in one of the traumatized communities of the north, where sexual violence against women and children was widespread, Mary would surely have been in the crosshairs of harm from within the region and trauma enacted from without.[14] For generations, Galilee bore the marks of trauma, and such abuse suffered by Mary could well have been one stain not mentioned in polite company.

A rumor arose years later from those familiar with the region about a possible relationship between Mary and a Roman soldier.[15] But it is closer to the truth of the time that soldiers were short on seduction and more given to brutality.[16] Galilee was known for "bastard children" of mixed-race origins due to the preponderance of soldiers and its proximity to foreigners. Maybe it wasn't an accident that, according to the Gospels, Jesus was confronted more than once about his questionable paternity. Though scandalous, such instances were known throughout the region.

The more history reveals about the experiences of women like Mary growing up in Galilee, the more we realize that hard times pressed on each family, sparing none.

What marks did young Mary's body bear? Was she surprised to be called "favored one" by Gabriel? Was it especially confusing because she knew a shame her body held? For a victim of abuse, it would have been all the more difficult to accept God's generous selection of her, and might have brought her to ask, *Why would God pick me?*

But here is Mary, a girl of Galilee in ways too hard to ponder for long. If the accusations that surrounded her and the region bore any truth, the God who goes to unexpected places—to the north, when all expect south; to lowly priests with no sons—this God can go to an unlikely girl in an unlikely place shaped by resistance and maybe even trauma. God shows favor, demonstrating again and again in infinite reversals that human taboo and stigma don't limit the Spirit.

◆ ◆ ◆

In 2017, I learned of Ahed Tamimi, a young girl from the small West Bank village of Nabi Saleh, northwest of Ramallah. She had been arrested for slapping an Israeli soldier. I watched, captivated, as her plight unfolded over the months of her detainment. When I turned to the pages of Luke's Gospel and the history of the Galilee region, I could not ignore the familiarity of these places, these stories.

In 1977, a settlement of Jewish families had taken up residence across the valley from Nabi Saleh, a place that I think has something of the look of Nazareth. It has been populated for three or four hundred years by one extended family, most carrying the Tamimi surname.[17] The settlement claimed the Tamimi family spring as their primary source of fresh water. Then they began to take much of the family's agricultural land, with the Israeli government's support. The result: incessant tension.

In 2009, Bassem Tamimi, an activist and one of the patriarchs of the community, began weekly protests. After Friday prayers at the mosque, he'd lead a march from the village square to the spring.

For the people of Nabi Saleh, the taking of the spring was a symbol of the Israeli occupation.[18] Their direct action was a way to confront the reality of their oppression. Each week, Israeli soldiers deployed tear gas, stun grenades, and rubber-coated bullets against the Palestinians. There were too many injuries to count, multiple arrests, and routine dousing with skunk water.[19] Bassem, his wife Nariman, and their four children suffered repeated raids of their home and harassment outside it. Every family was rocked by loss. Every family was traumatized by the occupation and protests. No one was free from conflict, no matter what their age.[20]

Whole families—even the children—protested. During the first Intifada, children across the region threw stones at Israeli soldiers.[21] During the second Intifada, the children of Nabi Saleh threw stones, snakes, and scorpions at the soldiers who harassed them daily in their village. They learned from their parents and grandparents some of the ways of resistance, developing a resolve not to accept the occupation as final or forever.

International activists and journalists who visited Nabi Saleh over the years asked about the participation of children. Wasn't it putting the children at risk? But Bassem and Nariman said the deeper challenge was that there was nowhere safe to hide the children from the violence of occupation. At least sharing in the weekly protests allowed them to learn to overcome their fears, giving them some small measure of agency. But, Nariman confessed, her own children struggled with nightmares, bedwetting, tantrums, and defiance at home.[22] The truth is that in fraught places, childhood is complex.

Ahed Tamimi, Bassem and Nariman's daughter, grew up marching. She was only ten when Mustafa, her cousin, was killed by soldiers. The following year, she witnessed the arrest of her mother (which she herself tried to stop) and then of her older brother. Her spine of steel hardened further over the years, and when soldiers came to her front yard after recently shooting another of her cousins in the face, she got close enough to land a slap. The next time the soldiers came, it was to take her to prison.

Ahed was sixteen when she was arrested.[23] Activist and poet Lisa Loden captured the scene: "Imprisoned, indicted / your short life already / a smoldering mountain of trauma, / loss, injustice ready to erupt . . . / Your narrow shoulders / bear the weight of generations / too heavy for your young flesh."[24]

Before she became an adult, Ahed became a Palestinian icon of resistance. It would be hard to argue that her life in Nabi Saleh didn't form her, that resistance wasn't fertile soil for her maturing resolve, and that the occupation didn't make her a rebel for justice's sake.

❖ ❖ ❖

We first meet Mary as an adolescent girl from Galilee. Like Ahed Tamimi, she was shaped by her place of origin. She saw soldiers riding into town, terrorizing her neighbors in the name of peacekeeping. She witnessed uncles humiliated and cousins hurt as a result of the soldiers' presence. She watched women taken by force to be punished in unspeakable ways. Maybe she knew their shame *too* well, on a personal level. But without a doubt, she experienced the push and pull of war and resistance that shaped the villages of Galilee.

Whether ancient Nazareth or modern Nabi Saleh, these places have formed young residents into rebels against imperial injustice. How could it be otherwise?

Then Gabriel visited Mary, insisted God favored her, already, early in her life. And before she could push against the imperial apparatus—or, like Ahed, in her own angry outburst, attack a solider with her fists—she was pulled into a peacemaking initiative by God's grace.

Violence, resistance, and trauma were formative forces for Mary, but they wouldn't be her whole story. Now, in the Spirit's overshadowing, the site of her trauma would become the locus of transformation. She would allow the most intimate, tender parts of herself to host incarnation's first inklings. Her body would become the *where* of incarnation as she trusted God as she could trust no other. From deep pain would now come *impossible* goodness for the world.

❖ ❖ ❖

"Behold!" the angel said to Mary, following all his assurances of favor. "Pay attention. Don't miss this," might be a better translation for our day. Gabriel told her she would conceive a son in the very folds of her body, she would name him Jesus, and he would be the Son of the Most High.[25] "This child," the angel continued, "will reign on King David's throne and over Jacob's house forever; he will have an unending kingdom."

The string of information about God's Son came at Mary fast. What she wanted to know first was, "How will this be?" Biblical scholar Jane Schaberg believes this to be a better translation than "How *can* this be?" as Mary pondered how it would be possible, given all that had happened to her. But God's power could overcome her humiliation.[26]

Gabriel answered that the Spirit would overshadow her. This is how she would conceive the Son of God.

Son of God? Only Caesar was called the son of God, the one who inaugurated world peace. If she was to believe the messenger, then she would give birth to a rival god, one able to contend with Caesar and reshape the world according to justice.

Maybe only a young rebel would be willing to accept such a mission.

"Behold!" the messenger said again. Another announcement. "Your once-barren relative, Elizabeth, is six months pregnant." God opens and overshadows wombs of both barren and virginal bodies for the birthing of a new kingdom.

Mary was catching on. Maybe she noticed the flavor of the Abrahamic tradition and remembered the once-barren Sarah—and recognized her in this new twist Elizabeth represented, if the messenger was to be trusted.

"For nothing will be impossible with God," Gabriel added. Nothing. Not erasing prejudice and animosity between the tribes in Galilee and Judea. Not establishing justice. Not defeating Rome. Not ending mass crucifixions, family separations, land confiscation, and lost inheritances. Not protecting women from beatings and rape by soldiers, and sexual abuse by neighbors and family members.[27]

Mary listened to the promise of the healing of so much hurt that had been visited on her people over the generations. "Behold!" she now said. With the confidence of a divine messenger, she announced her willingness to participate in God's plan. "I'm at God's service." Perhaps it was important that God asked her consent, when men did not.

And perhaps she agreed to become the locus for incarnation, knowing now that she could trust God with her very body. What kind of courage does it require for one battered by such an unforgiving landscape to say, "Behold"?

❖ ❖ ❖

The Church of the Annunciation in Nazareth stands as a testament to the seeds of courage Mary planted in that soil when she said yes to God's invitation. The basilica was built over the cave where, according to the tradition of the Catholic Church, Gabriel visited Mary. In the now-sizable city, the church is an anchor. Some call Nazareth "The Arab capital of Israel" because most of its residents are Arab citizens.[28] Nazareth—the place of migrants, of occupying forces, of constant motion. What remains, though, firmly rooted in the Galilean landscape, is the memory of Mary.

As I walked the courtyard of the church, I contemplated not only Jesus incarnated in Nazareth during the first advent but the ways in which he continues to be embodied today, in all nations. The courtyard displays artistic renderings of Mary from countries across the world. Most are the classic Madonna and Child motif, artwork from Guatemala, Ethiopia, Korea, Germany, and many other countries. Each one depicts Mary and her son in a manner reflecting the nation of origin. The rendering from Thailand shows Mary with a headdress and golden bangles. Scotland's portrayal has a fair-skinned mother and child complete with family crests. Spain offers Mary as a queen in ornate robes and a jewel-studded crown, holding Jesus in one hand and a diadem in the other.

People of each country imagine the Mother and Child as their kin, as members of their culture. I think of mothers and the children they hold—and try to keep holding—in places like Chile, the Philippines, and Greece, mothers practicing resistance and teaching their children to hunger for justice. I think of the sons and daughters of South Africa restoring equity to their land, the young people of Ireland reconciling north and south, and the next generation of Mexico maturing into revolutionaries in the humble spirit of the Mother of Guadalupe.

I imagine men and women in more and more places forging peace through nonviolence in the way of Jesus, wherever they are and however hard the terrain.

In this courtyard commemorating the place of Mary's first yes, I see images of the work of liberation, how it looks different in every context. But the origin story is here, in this cave-turned-courtyard.

❖ ❖ ❖

Mattathias, Zechariah, and Mary: good people who in their time were not necessarily considered exemplary. God has never been deterred by the ordinariness of people. High rank, economic security, and pristine sexuality weren't necessary for practitioners of peace in God's campaign. Everyday people—a village priest and a girl from Galilee—conversed with an angel.

And hard places are the places of the first advent: occupied Judea, feral Galilee, an insignificant village like

Nazareth. God's peace was unfurled where life wasn't working, where people hurt most, where hope was on the run. *Here*, God declared, *here, peace can—here, peace will—bloom.*

4

MOTHERS OF ADVENT

Mary and Elizabeth
Ein Kerem | Luke 1:39–56

The small village of Ein Kerem sits just outside Jerusalem, green and terraced from centuries of agriculture. Tradition remembers this place as the home of Zechariah and Elizabeth and the birthplace of John the Baptist. It is also the place to which Mary soon traveled after the messenger Gabriel's announcement and assurances. She needed her elder relative now—and reprieve from gossip in Galilee.

Today the site is commemorated by the Church of the Visitation, which echoes that terraced landscape with a lower church and courtyard and an upper chapel with a high-reaching ceiling pulling visitors' attention upward. Ein Kerem brims with churches and chapels, icons and grottos, but this place honors two women who visited together while incubating God's advent as the world carried on unaware.

The upper chapel brings together an homage to Mother Mary and the witness of other iconic women of

Israel, including Deborah, Jael, and Judith. For the Christian pilgrim, what place these peripheral women have in Mary's chapel can be a conundrum.

The lower church centers the pilgrim back in the story of two mothers, two pregnancies, and two announced sons. A mosaic portrays the elder and younger relatives reaching for one another. There is a sense of anticipation of Elizabeth's "Hail, Mary!"—her first greeting of the young girl when she arrived at Elizabeth and Zechariah's home. The courtyard is surrounded with tiled tributes to Mary's advent song, which is recorded in the first chapter of Luke's Gospel and later became known as the Magnificat.[1] In the courtyard, this song is translated into forty-two languages. And at the entry to the courtyard, visitors are greeted by a patinated statue of the women simply embracing. One woman's body clearly shows the bulge of the child within, the other not. In the sculpture, they hold a somber gaze at this beginning moment of their visit, before advent revelations unfurl. Here we witness the mothers of advent together for the first time.

❖　❖　❖

Mary hurried to the hills of Judea to meet her relative, not only because Gabriel had announced Elizabeth's pregnancy but with a rush of eagerness to talk with someone who might share Mary's questions, confusion, and hopes. Did she also hurry because she was scared about her precarious condition?[2] As she made her way into the Judean hills, perhaps she had to push through the prejudice of southerners looking down on her kind. She traveled there despite the added stigma of arriving at the door of a priest's home as a pregnant and unwed woman.[3] It was a small grace that she wasn't showing yet.

As Mary entered Zechariah's house, Elizabeth greeted her with words her husband still lacked. During the call-and-response of greetings between the women, Elizabeth felt her baby leap in her womb, and she was filled with the Holy Spirit. According to Luke's telling, the instantaneous impartation unleashed Elizabeth to give a prophetic utterance naming the significance of the moment: "Blessed are you among women," she said, "and blessed is the fruit of your womb!"[4]

Her words echoed Jewish tradition and history: the warrior-judge Deborah and her pronouncement over Jael. Elizabeth's words reverberated also with notes from Judith's triumph recounted in the Apocrypha. Both of these extraordinary, valiant women had delivered Israel in the heat of battle, rising to the challenge of their fraught times. In the fog of war, Deborah and Judith did what the men could not do: act decisively amid disarray. Their stories are told in the books of Judges and Judith, respectively.[5] Songs were written about them, narratives told again and again about their valor and ability to outwit enemy warriors with the courageous and clever use of female power.[6]

These women had another commonality amid crisis—they engaged in violence.[7] Deborah, leader of the military campaign, sings Jael's praises. Her song does not shy away from the graphic details of Jael's victorious kill, driving a tent peg into the skull of the enemy, Sisera. The victory song is perhaps the oldest recorded in the Hebrew Bible, making a song composed by and about a woman the true original.[8] Jewish lore from a later period echoes that first song in the account of Judith beheading Holofernes, another general. Smuggling his severed head out of the enemy camp, she returns to her own and shows the prize to cowering (male) Israelite soldiers.[9] Both women crossed the lines of traditional roles. Both killed. Both were celebrated, the violence notwithstanding. "Blessed are you among women" is the refrain for these noble women that was now repeated in the Judean hills.

Elizabeth's reprisal comes as a glorious twist, since Mary will embody nonviolent participation in the advent of God's peace. And Elizabeth's verse will add a new understanding of deliverance, opening space for women in the future to engage tumultuous times anew to effect change. Everyone who heard the song's beginning would assume they knew how it ended. But Elizabeth and Mary, under the auspices of the Spirit, understood the song as pointing in a new direction. Advent ushered in a new era in which women are blessed for their acts of peace, not participation in violence.[10]

Elizabeth and Mary followed in the tradition of Israel's matriarchs, engaging in the political realities of their time. In ancient Roman Palestine, religious, political, and economic life blended together. When women acted in public space, their action was as political as it was religious and economic. They stood and sang with Deborah, who was called the Mother of Israel—a political title.[11] They stood with Jael and Judith, warriors delivering victory in national battles. They sang with Miriam, an organizer for liberation from slavery alongside Moses and Aaron. They sang with women like Hannah, whose songs created a common vocabulary for resistance, lament, and victory. Standing with and for others was all of a piece in the Israelite imagination.

❖ ❖ ❖

When Elizabeth saw Mary, she knew her to be in the company of the iconic women of Israelite history. She recognized that God's spirit was creating messianic newness in her womb. When Mary, not yet showing, told her about the visit from the angel Gabriel and the overshadowing of the Spirit, Elizabeth listened and believed her. In her song, she affirmed the work of God in her young Galilean relative.

Elizabeth confessed that at the sound of Mary's voice, the baby in her own womb had leapt with joy[12]—another kind of bodily affirmation of God's work among them.

Maybe they laughed together at the audacity of God with *them*, of all people. As descendants of Mother Sarah, maybe their holy hilarity was a reversal of her laughter tinged with disbelief.[13] These two women believed: Elizabeth believed Mary. Mary believed Gabriel's words. And Mary's elder relative called her blessed once again.

You can never hear those words enough amid times of uncertainty and fresh revelation. Standing in the courtyard of The Visitation with two dear friends on a crisp, clear day, I experienced that truth in my own body. We were surrounded with the words of Mary's Magnificat in the courtyard of many languages, encircled by this refrain of her song, in response to the blessing from Elizabeth. We contemplated together the fresh meaning of these words, one friend speaking from her history living in the region and walking the Ein Kerem hills often, the other unfolding how this encounter between Mary and Elizabeth nourished her own imagination. In that courtyard, as I listened to my friends inviting me into a blessed space akin to that of our advent matriarchs, I was given courage and companionship for the theological work at hand. They poured into me as I was working through these texts, the testimony of these very women. We climbed the stairs to the chapel and sat before a fresco of Mother Mary; we wondered about the influence of Judith, Jael, and Deborah in Mary's words. And to this day, the spirit of these ancient women infuses my cherished friendships, my understanding of the matriarchs.

The incarnation conversations between Mary and Elizabeth were conceived in listening, trust, and shared belief. Imagine these women talking as they did household chores together, took walks to and from the village well, and prepared meals side by side. Conversations not just about Sarah but about other women, like Samuel's mother Hannah, and Joseph's mother Rachel. Their God opened wombs to life. Elizabeth understood her former barrenness and the new life forming as part of a successive line with these matriarchs. Another sort of divine work was forming in Mary, both agreed. God's Holy Self had taken residence in her and reversed her humiliation.

Their sons would change the world as they knew it, and from their songs it was clear that the sons would do things differently. A series of reversals had shown both of them that. There must have been conversations about what it might look like to raise revolutionary men who would be part of deliverance, ending war rather than contributing to its incessant cycles. And what might justice look like for Judea and Galilee?—since it seemed obvious to them now that God would include both regions in the future peace. How would their motherhood be different from others', given their extraordinary sons? Would they know greater glory or greater hardship? Would God growing up among them bring immediate or gradual change?

As Elizabeth and Mary conversed, Zechariah listened. Their discussions ranged from the most practical to the most intimate kind of theology he'd ever heard. As he heard sacred stories anew, their insights showed him their capacity for rigorous theological reflection related to their lives, their land. But hearing them muse aloud about incarnation, an unthinkable concept before Gabriel's visit, might have astounded him. Apparently, the women in his life were quick to believe and quick to innovate with the Spirit. Those epiphanies would render his silence golden.

Within Advent's testimony are two women leading the conversation about God's groundbreaking work among us.[14] As Elizabeth and Mary worked to understand what was happening in their bodies, they dreamed the possibility of new horizons of God's action in troubled landscapes. Their living theology fueled revolutions and peace movements.

❖ ❖ ❖

Mary didn't fight; Mary sang. She stood in the tradition of Deborah, wise judge and mighty warrior, singer of the oldest song in scripture. She channeled the canticles of Hannah and Judith and the mother of liberation, Miriam.[15] Following in the footsteps of her ancestors, she composed laments, victory songs, and the range of traditional choruses in between. Songs were her work of resistance, her response to the injustice she witnessed and likely suffered in Nazareth.

The memories of the exodus from Egypt and the daily experiences of life in Galilee shaped Mary's resistance refrains. Accordingly, she wove lyrics together with lament and imprecatory heat. Other verses she filled with praise or gratitude or messianic hope. Pleas for deliverance were common in her songbook. Both trauma and liberation were hallmarks of her hymns. If trauma could be transformed into songs, maybe song could be a part of diminishing the deep distress of Galilean life.

Most likely, villagers knew some sacred stories, some psalms and parables from the oral tradition of their culture, but few read or studied all of the holy words. It took time for stories and songs to move among networks of regional villages and to pass down through families. So Mary in Nazareth began with a handful of old songs circulating in her community, maybe a few from her mother, Anna. Maybe she rehearsed them as she journeyed from Nazareth to Judea's hills and Ein Kerem.[16]

In the three months Mary spent with Elizabeth, they would have talked about Elizabeth's descendancy from the priestly line of Aaron, and of Mary's lineage. Perhaps there were songs Elizabeth taught her—old songs new to Mary. And perhaps Elizabeth helped her learn not only the words of the old songs but also the meanings and histories attached to them. They would have searched and learned together from the matriarchs of Israel, about their suffering and survival and even joys amid struggle.

Together, Elizabeth and Mary reflected on the words of their sacred traditions and likely considered how they embodied the witness of their predecessors now, in their current landscape.

The story would continue with them.

When Elizabeth called Mary blessed, in the words of Deborah's praise of Jael, it wasn't only the song but the solidarity between the women that pierced Mary's young heart. Grafted into generations of women practicing liberation through subversive songs and solidarity, Mary was formed by song, and then she composed song, creating a legacy, weaving herself into the unwritten genealogy of women who birthed the sons and daughters of Israel. She came to see her place among her people, singing, "From now on all generations will call me blessed." And as she sang of God's goodness toward her, she sang also of generations before who met God's mercy. And she sang for generations to come.[17] Hers was no solitary song, but a prophetic chorus born of solidarity with many matriarchs, and with Emmanuel, working salvation even now through her.

But the song was personal; it sprouted from her own reversal. In the Magnificat of Luke, Mary sings of her low estate, a status typically translated as "poor" or "humble." But there is a fuller connotation to this word, *tapeinōsis*, that refers to humiliation or distress. And this can be seen earlier in the Hebrew Bible, as the word is used to connote the sexual humiliation of Dinah, the concubine in Judges 19, and King David's daughter Tamar, to name just a few. It might even be that Luke's use of this word in Mary's song is an intertextual nod to a passage in Deuteronomy, where the law directs response in handling the seduced or sexually humiliated betrothed virgin.[18] What if Mary sings of her own humiliation and God's astounding redemption of her shame in this present moment? Instead of punishment, blessing? What if she sings as the first fruit of God's grand reversal? What if she goes on to sing of God exalting the other humiliated ones with such confidence because she has already experienced the beginning of such holy upheaval herself?[19]

Mary's anthem tells of those brutalized by the empire, literally and metaphorically, who will know God's recompense. Liberation will overcome humiliation and stigma; God's justice will have the final victorious word for those like her in the world. Mary understands that her own experience of reversal will be shared with all the meek ones. And her song will set a trajectory for the future, where her humiliation is transformed into incarnation in a way that foreshadows how her son's death by imperial crucifixion, another humiliation, will be transformed by resurrection. This God of Mary's song upends all the empire's violent tactics.

With her advent song composed in the hills of Judea, Mary forged a new resistance movement. The Magnificat grew from her time with Elizabeth, from their conversations and robust singing as they walked the uneven roads of Ein Kerem side by side. As their bellies grew, so too did their convictions about God's coming deliverance. No surprise then that Mary bursts out with this song, braiding together songs of old with her new understanding of God's work and celebrating God's mighty deeds among the meek, like herself and her community. With boldness, Mary declares an astonishing reversal in which the proud will be confused and the mighty dethroned, while the humble ones will be elevated to those vacated positions. Her song envisions a world order where the village elders, once trampled by menacing soldiers and crooked politicians, are vindicated. Local leaders will finally manage their own affairs with equity. The hungry, her neighbors in Nazareth among them, will be seated at tables full of good food. They will be able to savor the bounty from their own fields, the fruits of their own labor. And the rich, who gained their wealth through exploitation of her neighbors, will be sent away with empty pockets, now experiencing the pangs of poverty in this reversal of empire economics.

Mary sings out a new social order that upends the status quo as advent begins to turn tables on those who benefit from the injustice of empires and their economies— long before her own son would himself overturn tables, enacting protest in the temple.[20]

Some songs soothe; others become subversive anthems to galvanize radical hope and future action. The song Mary sang was one of change already afoot.

❖ ❖ ❖

Together, Elizabeth and Mary, the mothers of advent, shaped the infrastructure of peace. Their bodies, metaphors within the songs they sang, spoke about newness God was birthing into the world. In their flourishing friendship, they collaborated to create and embody novel paradigms. They spoke about possibilities and limitations, challenging one another and allowing hope to generate. Together, they did the work of theology, in cooperation and communal engagement, gestating God's peace, which reversed the unjust order.

So many of the hymns composed during the Maccabean Revolt sang of nationalistic salvation, of revenge and violence. But the mothers of advent teach about disarming in the move toward God's justice. In Mary's advent anthem, we see no vindictiveness.[21] And we find that same spirit in future years in her son, when in the synagogue he reads from the scroll of Isaiah the words of jubilee announced there but omits the words of wrath. In the advent trajectory set by his mother to reverse unjust structures, not with a spirit of revenge but restoration, Jesus followed.[22]

In the company of women peacemakers in Israel and Palestine, I hear ancient cadences in work for justice. Muslim, Jewish, and Christian women all sing of a future birthed by nonviolence, love, and justice for all who call the land home. Some have suffered the loss of children to the violence of occupation or the resistance, yet they come together in their grief to lament even as they compose new songs of hope. Others make music with their feet as they march, arm in arm, to demonstrate the desire for justice across their landscape. Still, other mothers share laughter like a song as they make jam, not conflict, together.[23] Their songs are contagious and keep the lyrics of liberation alive in me.

❖ ❖ ❖

By the end of their third month together, Mary's child barely showed in the gentle slope of incarnational goodness in her belly. Enfolded in her flesh, God had started stretching her skin early—stretching, too, her concept of God's deliverance across both Galilee and Judea. As the turbulence of her terrain raged, she became a testament not just to resistance but to resilience. Her heart beat for a justice that made any stigma she would bear an acceptable cost, for peace would come to her community—and beyond.

Amid taboo, gossip, and misunderstandings, Mary stood. She had agreed to be seen as an unwed mother, to risk disgrace among her community in order to birth hope. Surviving stigma and struggle was her experience, and it became part of the DNA of her son.

Among the many things advent reveals, one is that you can't save what you don't experience or intimately know. Jesus would grow up with stigma of his own: as a Galilean, a Nazorean tradesman, and "Mary's son," as some referred to him, snidely calling his paternity into question.[24] Before becoming a savior, he would be a survivor, not unlike his own mother.

❖ ❖ ❖

As Mary returned to Nazareth, to Joseph, and to all that would challenge her there, she came with a song. And it was a song that also remained with Elizabeth, who soon gave birth to a son. The family and the entire neighborhood came out to rejoice with her, just as they had with Mother Sarah.[25]

When the day of circumcision came, inducting the newborn into the faith of Israel, everyone expected a long tradition to continue: that the child would be named after his father. But Elizabeth shocked them all when she stepped in and named him John. She confounded those gathered because none of their relatives, no one in their tribal heritage, had that name.

Bewildered, everyone looked to Zechariah to confirm the naming of the child. He asked for a tablet and wrote, "His name is John."[26] Then the stunned silence that followed was broken: at last, Zechariah spoke! He began blessing God, even as fear overcame those listening to him. Word soon traveled across the hillside of Judea, and some who heard the news of the unorthodox birth announcement pondered it in their hearts.[27] This son, unexpected name and all, generated fresh expectations among Zechariah's kin.

Meanwhile, Zechariah—not unlike Elizabeth and Mary—erupted into song. Yes, he sang of his newborn son! But his hymn, known now as the Benedictus, focused on God's deliverance of Israel from all enemies. This redemption song celebrated God's might and mercy to the generations since Abraham. What's more, Zechariah anticipated new political freedom, even economic relief, for his neighbors.[28] In this moment, he knew that God's goodness was not just about his son, but about all the sons and daughters of Israel who waited for God's arrival.

Those three months of the mothers in spirit-breathed conversation and song under Zechariah's roof were an intimate part of his transformation. In his silence, he had listened to them. He had allowed their holy curiosity to provoke his own. Their wrestling with generational wisdom shaped him in ways he had never before experienced in the company of the temple priests. These women energized his faith with their own. Perhaps he was the first to be mothered by their advent goodness.

The impartation of the Spirit, the incarnation musings, and a fresh kind of solidarity were among the gifts planted by Mary's visit to the soil of Ein Kerem. Those seed-gifts would start to grow before she even returned to Nazareth. And in the footsteps of Deborah, Mary began mothering Israel with her advent anthem.

Now, when you walk into the courtyard of the Church of the Visitation, the site of the origin of Zechariah's transformation, you are still greeted by Mary's words of grand reversal. In dozens of languages, her song continues for traumatized lands in unison with her heart and hope.

❖ ❖ ❖

Lisa Loden, first mentioned in chapter 3, lives in the northern part of Israel. I met her one night in Jerusalem among a variety of women from the region who work together for peace. Introduced by a mutual friend, we quickly discovered another friend in common: Emmanuel Katongole.[29] We talked about his work on reconciliation, which matched our own hearts for the same. Over soup and salmon, despite differing national, generational, and faith traditions, we found an instant kinship.

We talked about theology and the land. Lisa mentioned that she was an autodidact, dedicated to self-study of theology regarding justice, peace, and reconciliation. But that night as we spoke, surrounded by women at work for peace, I didn't realize she was a member of a minority community in Israel, often maligned and misunderstood: she is an Israeli Messianic Jew.[30] I learned that Jewish people have no easy category for a Jew who believes in Jesus as Messiah. There is a strong stigma attached to Lisa's identity. As we grew in friendship, I often thought of her in the Galilee region, like Mary, considered by many Israelis to be a lesser Jew or not a Jew at all.

Lisa and her husband, David, immigrated to Israel in the 1970s. They've pastored communities, shaping theology around Messianic understandings. But even within her own community, Lisa is considered an anomaly because of her perspective on justice for all the people of the land—Jews and Palestinians alike.

In her rigorous study of scripture over the years, Lisa grew more committed to peace, and soon it became central in her writing, teaching, poetry, and activism. In 2016 she participated in the March of Hope led by Women Wage Peace, traveling with diverse women who hunger for peace in their land.[31] From the Jordan River to Jerusalem, thousands of mothers marched "for a better future, for another way, for an end to violence, bloodshed, and terror."[32] The women sang together in Arabic, Hebrew, and English to "bring down the peace, bring down the peace."[33]

Fewer than five women from the Messianic community joined in the march, Lisa noted. She could easily have felt alone. But while she felt sadness at her community's absence, she experienced something as ancient and true as the meeting between Mary and Elizabeth: solidarity with sisters who shared her heart for peace.

Because of Lisa's commitment to God's generous justice on behalf of both Israelis and Palestinians, many who don't understand her have called her a traitor. She's suffered the loss of intimate friendships. For now, she stands, like Elizabeth, in the theological gap between the old traditions and a new way she hopes will dawn. In kinship, she has had to stand among her own community and name the uneasy truth. Wherever she goes, she seeks solidarity among other peacemakers and embodies an advent faith.

Embodying the familiar echoes of both Mary and Elizabeth, Lisa joins with all the other mothers of generations from past to present in showing us that change is possible, singing and marching together for a peace— God's peace—rooted in justice.

❖ ❖ ❖

Across a landscape awash in war, occupation, and trauma, Elizabeth proclaimed Mary's blessedness. She spoke of solidarity in the face of an empire determined to bend women like them. Into this stream, Mary sang her Magnificat of striking reversals in her own life and in the structure of society. Together, they would mother peacemakers and revolutionaries for millennia to come.

They were two women with seemingly little influence in their world. But what they did, according to Luke, was as significant as joining in the start of a new world order, organized by God's justice and lived in God's peace.

5

A HOSPITABLE BIRTH IN A HARD ECONOMY

Caesar's Census, Jesus's Birth

Bethlehem | Luke 2:1–7

Behind the separation wall on Star Street in Bethlehem is an economy tied to hospitality in ways that overlap the first advent, when Mary and Joseph journeyed south to this town under Caesar's census. Star Street is the traditionally acknowledged final portion of that journey. Even imperial demands don't stamp out resistance and neighborliness— the way families look out for one another. It is how those imperiled by the empire and its exploitive economics persevere: hospitality is how people honor the humanity of one another on the underside of the empire.

My husband, Claude, and I traveled to Bethlehem. My first vivid memory of the place is of Star Street. As we walked the advent road, we were met by a local man carrying a round brass tray, offering us hot tea with a fierce and repeated insistence. We swerved up limestone stairs to sidestep his hounding hospitality, uneasy with his incessant pursuit. Later, however, we returned to sit in the alley by the blue metal door of his kiosk. What we had perceived as the desperation of economic need on the part of the local tea vendor actually represented a more complex reality. The Bethlehemite economy was wracked by the separation wall and checkpoints created by the Israeli government, making it harder for tourists to visit, stay, and spend money in the little town of world renown.

Many pilgrims stay away from Bethlehem for fear of crossing a checkpoint into the West Bank. If they do go, they spend four hours instead of four days, bringing with them fears of Palestinian violence. Rushed in by tour guides only to visit the Church of the Nativity and a few select shops for souvenirs, they then board their tour bus and hurry out.

But that would be to miss the taste of Sami's tea, Afteem's falafel, and fresh-squeezed pomegranate juice in Manger Square. Nor in their haste would such tourists have taken time to notice the minarets next to the church spires—and to learn the story these tell about this place. Tourism risks seeing the holy sites through a narrow lens that often does not introduce visitors to the people who have stewarded these sites with care for centuries as an aspect of fidelity to their homeland.

If we glance too quickly at Joseph and Mary's journey south to Bethlehem, we miss the economic hardship that permeates the advent scene. And the vibrant life that also surrounds it.

I sometimes wonder if we are afraid to truly see them for fear of what that encounter might demand of us.

As pilgrims, my husband and I came with different expectations. As visitors in a foreign land, we were treated as guests. We were guests who gave time to listen to Bethlehemite stories, even as we supported the community in a small way, by bringing dollars to a struggling economy. It felt like more than a fair trade—like we received more than we gave.

Behind the separation wall, we experienced kindness and joy, a kind of abundance we won't soon forget. And this Bethlehem visit opened the door for consideration about what it means to visit hard places and be a pilgrim in solidarity with local people, rather than a tourist.

Our interaction with the locals showed us that even innkeepers need to eat, purveyors of tea have school fees to pay for their children, shopkeepers have medical bills to settle. Mutuality is part of hospitality—we are given a room, a meal, and the opportunity in return to offer money that will infuse the local economy and allow for provisions for our hosts. In depressed economies, our dollars are a tangible sign of support. Sami's welcome was genuine—he also needed us to buy his tea. Both facts are true and common in stingy economies where people struggle to survive. And both reflect something of the

advent story in Luke about the overlap of uneven economies and hospitality among the poor ones, like Joseph
and Mary.

❖ ❖ ❖

The whole world, now under the control of Caesar, met a
decree to register for Rome's census. It would be the first
such registration under the Syrian governor, a client ruler
in the region. And everyone in the empire went to their
ancestral hometown to register. This meant that Joseph
had to go from Galilee south to Judea, from Nazareth to
the root system of his family tree, Bethlehem, to register.
Mary, in her very pregnant state, had to travel the rutted
terrain with him.[1] When Caesar spoke, everyone moved.

Luke sets the advent scene with an unmistakable
economic marker—the census. Caesar's census was not
about demographic numbers; it was a count of livestock,
crops, and people who could pay taxes.[2] It was an inventory of wealth that allowed the empire to further spread
the burden of taxation. A census was always bad news for
the poor, never lightening their load. From time to time,
though, a census was known to ignite rebellion.[3]

In the opening verses of Luke 2, the most complete
advent narrative in scripture, the word *register* or *registration* appears four times in quick succession. Ancient readers would know that meant the land was preoccupied
with taxation. Enrollment in the census to "pay tribute"

(taxes) to Rome was the immediate context of this scene. The tax initiative reached from Syria down to Judea and from the rulers, like Caesar and Quirinius, to the ruled, like Joseph and Mary. No one was spared, not a single villager.

Luke doesn't provide an exact history so much as he creates a picture of the world Jesus was born into: economic hardship, a reign of power. The implications were that things were tight—and would soon get tighter as Caesar calculated the tribute owed to him and his functionaries (provincial rulers and high priests included). And as everyone knew, to not pay tribute equaled rebellion and invited the punishment of Roman legions.[4] Caesar's economy was precarious and potentially perilous for most, including Joseph and Mary.

Luke refrains from saying much about Joseph in his advent narrative, giving preference to Mary's perspective. We will have to wait for Matthew's telling to reveal more about how Joseph experienced the arrival of their son. What Luke does in his gospel, here and throughout, is open more space for the voices of women. In a patriarchal society, this is no small move. He centers the experience of women, engaging them as integral to conversations about faith and discipleship. He begins with Mary and Elizabeth. The narrative of men could be assumed; the one focusing on the women was more than just a rhetorical choice—it was a subversive reversal.

Imperial fiat: one word, a single order from a seat of power, and populations shifted without recourse. A census is impersonal and mandatory. Luke points with a heavy hand at the census and registration, to highlight not only the economy but also migration patterns. In addition, it points to family trees and roots. No exceptions, not even for a woman whose child is nearly crowning.

History does not corroborate the kind of census described by Luke, where people were required to return to ancestral towns to enroll in order to pay taxes. Imperial administrations counted and calculated what they could extract. There is a census connected to Quirinius, but at a date after the birth of Jesus.[5] But again, Luke creates a world that mimics the dynamics he and his audience experienced, enfolding this advent story into something bigger than one moment in time. It is about both the first advent and all the times God arrives into our conflicted lands and broken economies.

That Luke's focus begins with the economy and ever-looming loss shows us an economic world with all its demands, exploitation, and humiliation for those at the bottom. Against this backdrop of taxation, salvation entered. And the kind of deliverance Luke suggests is one that deals with realities like the hunger for daily bread, fear of land loss, the search for work, and the burden of indebtedness.

❖ ❖ ❖

Joseph and Mary made their way from Nazareth to Bethlehem as the empire and its economy demanded. They found long-lost family members awaiting them, and they squeezed in where they could. According to the logic of Luke's narrative, the small town was full of Nazoreans and others from across Roman Palestine returning home. Neighborhoods surged with the influx of relatives coming to register, and every corner of every house hosted someone. Bethlehemites worked to make room for everyone—Joseph and Mary were no exception.

Some Nazorean families had never been south at all since the long-ago time when their ancestors returned from Babylonian exile and stopped in Nazareth or other northern villages. For some, this was their first chance to connect with southern relatives and perhaps their initial contact with the landscape that nourished Jesse and was home to King David. The excitement of reunions mingled in the air alongside economic anxiety and the census, a form of communal joy functioning as resistance to imperial edicts.

Those who returned entered common Bethlehemite houses built like simple compounds with a series of small structures arranged around a stall where the livestock stayed at night.[6] Some covered rooms ringed the stall, and beyond that were a few private, enclosed rooms where most of the family lived.

But that left plenty of space to offer guests between private and semi-private places within the family compound.

What Luke describes is a full house, the private enclosures full and even the covered rooms unavailable. By the time the couple arrived, the only room available was a corner in the open stall area among the livestock, where a manger stood. Still, this was within the family compound, and inside, they would have met the warmth of expected hospitality.

Most Advent scenes we construct misunderstand the scenario that greeted Joseph, Mary, and many others upon their arrival. They were welcomed by family. However, we are told "there was no room for them in the inn," a phrase better understood as "there was no space for them in the usual guest room of the home."[7] Room was made for everyone, even if it was a corner here or a stable there. As long as everyone was under the same roof, it didn't matter if they were in a private nook or on a straw mat next to the goats.

We are not invited into any family discussions about Joseph's wife or any shame her circumstance might have presented locally. If his kin felt the sting of her stigma or any unease at hosting her, Luke leaves it unspoken. Joseph's acceptance of her, which we will learn more of from Matthew's gospel, stood. All the family could do was follow his lead and make space for her, despite any discomfort of their own. But then again, Mary's situation would not have been unfamiliar. Joseph's response was the unexpected twist, as far as the family might be concerned.

The home was bursting at the seams, but Joseph and Mary would have still been around the table for meals, and still joining in the conversations among relatives. Modern notions of private spaces had no place in the ancient rubric. Every relative received welcome. And everyone adjusted to make it work.

❖ ❖ ❖

Amid the bustle of family and all the related logistics of accommodating everyone, Mary's water broke. Maybe she was among the other women preparing the evening meal, chopping cucumbers or pitting olives, when the cooks transformed into midwives. They guided her to the corner of the stall and made room for her to lie down and for them to huddle round her for the duration of labor. Dinner could wait; the baby might not.

So Mary experienced the birth of her first child, not alone with only Joseph to help, but surrounded by mothers and midwives. She was grateful Elizabeth had arrived the day before, that she could rely on her company once again as they crossed another threshold together. She drew from the wisdom of her relatives as she gripped their hands. She let out screams that startled the goats and made the donkey, still tired from the long journey, anxious. Mary's son—God's Son—crowned. In that moment, no one thought of Caesar or the registration or the coming tax increase. A new life entered the world.

Mary and Elizabeth thought that perhaps a new kingdom had entered too.

This birth of the prince of God's peace changed the world. Against the harsh backdrop of an imperial economy, he came into the world in the most common circumstances. He embodied the hopes of ordinary priests and farmers for true liberation; he confronted the fears they carried that life would only get worse for them under this empire. "The hopes and fears of all the years were met"[8] in the holy child as God took direct action and entered the story in human skin.

❖ ❖ ❖

Is there any hospitality on offer in Bethlehem? This is one of the conversations around Joseph and Mary's arrival to their ancestral home and, soon after, the birth of their child. Due to poor interpretation of Luke's text, Bethlehem and her innkeepers have historically been burdened with a bad reputation regarding their lack of hospitality for the Holy Family.

Fadi Kattan is both innkeeper and chef at the Hosh al-Syrian Guest House. As a Bethlehemite, he is familiar with the caricature of the inhospitable innkeeper from Luke's brief mention in his narrative. "It's contrary to what I know of Palestinians—we are so open to foreigners and guests," he said as we spoke of that first advent. He assured me that his fellow innkeepers would never turn away a pregnant woman or any woman in distress, then or now. Then he added that the Abrahamic faith traditions shaped the local practice of hospitality: a welcome extended to all guests, foreigners, and travelers.[9]

The misreading of Luke's text, mixed with logistic challenges presented by life behind the separation wall, makes it easy for people to misunderstand who the original witnesses to the birth of Jesus in Bethlehem might have been. They were the people of the land, some of whom might have been Chef Fadi's ancestors. And today's Palestinian Christians still commemorate the arrival of Joseph and Mary down the cobbled Star Street and celebrate the birth of Bethlehem's favorite son. Jesus was born into the extended welcome of Jewish relatives and Palestinian neighbors, living stones who bear witness to Jesus in their hometown.[10] Chef Fadi reminds me that the original welcome continues on the part of the Palestinian community. "We are still here," he says.

❖ ❖ ❖

In the logic of Luke's narrative there is another scenario. When families were called to pay tribute, every family member helped bring in the harvest needed to pay their share. Families would spread out in orchards to harvest fruits, nuts, or olives. They'd crowd together under the generous canopy of fig trees at mealtime to share bread and sage tea. The family presence would make clear that this land was not abandoned or easy pickings for the imperial interlopers. Yes, a large portion of their bounty

would be given over for taxes. But their presence somehow embodied a kind of resistance. They were still here.
They could be moved by imperial decree, but not easily
erased from their land.

In the advent story, as Luke tells it, the economy matters. Attentive readers are led to understand a concrete
kind of pressure, which also sets tangible contours for
that expectant hope. Against the backdrop of a danger-
ously exploitive economy, what does deliverance look
like? Debt relief? Debt forgiveness? Lighter tax burden?
Ample economic resources to avoid foreclosure, to keep
family land? Are these a part of God's salvation?

A deeper understanding of the economics of advent
shows us that beyond our consumer-driven season's gifts
for one another, a more profound investigation is called
for of our economy and how it impinges on our neighbors. Luke's text asks: Do we see who is crushed by the
current economic realities? Do we understand that even
our acts of charity are too thin against the demands of
advent? Because there must be more than benefiting from
Caesar's economy all year long and then giving from our
extra during one short season. There must be more than
our deciding which people in need we deem worthy of
our generosity.

A true resistance worthy of the first advent would
be a move into durable justice work the rest of the year.
Imagine giving to a local food bank during Advent and
then working on advocacy related to food insecurity and

childhood hunger the rest of the year. Imagine learning about the realities around school lunch programs—how many need free or reduced-price lunches in your local schools; whether quality meals are offered—and organizing your community to improve what is on offer to kids. Imagine spending the year tackling the policies that create food deserts, which keep many neighborhoods undernourished. But there are many other possibilities: affordable housing and tenants' rights, fair wages, accessible healthcare and medications, or indigenous land rights.

When I think of how Luke puts the economy front and center in his advent narrative, I imagine that we are meant to do the same in our present Advent practice. How do we see the economy, who it hurts, and how its structures are riddled with injustice? What do we do to come alongside the modern Josephs and Marys, forced to move to Bethlehem and suffer the modern Caesar's unforgiving tax burden? Offering hospitality to those crushed by economic hardship, yes. But also hearing Mary's song echo in our ears and move us to participate in a grand reversal that feeds the hungry and dethrones those who dominate the economy for their own benefit.

For Luke, the economy is no mere backdrop for the narrative; it's a feature of a deeper engagement with the reality of the world God arrives to upend for the sake of justice and peace.

❖ ❖ ❖

You only have to visit Bethlehem once for the notion of an inhospitable innkeeper to be deconstructed. Tea vendors like Sami, taxi drivers like Naïef, restaurateurs like Chef Fadi Kattan, and a bevy of shopkeepers along Star Street beckon visitors to come and see. They obviously have things to sell—it is their livelihood, after all. So there is reason for them to welcome visitors. But this isn't crass economics; it is also vocation and generations of family life sustained in similar ways. There is a warmth among Bethlehemites, an eagerness to share their beloved town with visitors and tell stories about their lives. Stories you do not want to miss when walking Star Street or visiting with locals.

Claude and I checked into Hosh al-Syrian, Chef Fadi's small guest house carved into a limestone building dating back to the 1700s, finally settling into the charm of Bethlehem. "If you want the best tea in Bethlehem, stop by and meet Sami," the innkeeper recommended. And that is how we found our way back to the insistent tea vendor mere steps away from our inn.

A tattered blue awning marked the cut-out kitchen, kettle whistling, herbs piled high. When he saw us, a smile overtook his face as he offered tea. He pulled out plastic chairs and a small table. "Sit, sit," he instructed. He appeared again with glass mugs of steaming tea with rosemary, cardamom pods, and a lime wedge. He sat with us and told stories unsolicited. "My mother is Christian, my father is Muslim, but I just love everyone," he said.

And sitting in his makeshift café, listening to the dueling sounds of the call to prayer and a riot of church bells, it made sense.

Over Sami's stove hung a printed picture, in a plastic sleeve, of him cheek to cheek with Conan O'Brien, his favorite American. Sami spoke about the antics that landed him on the comedy show, acting them out with enthused animation. He leaned in and shared how the comedian made time to listen and ask good questions. When he learned of a substantial need in the tea vendor's family, he gave tangible assistance that Sami will never stop celebrating. We learned that Sami didn't love the man's celebrity so much as his generosity and kindness.

He told the story of a man who took an interest in him over another cup of tea upon hearing of the struggle Sami and his wife had starting their family. He was an Israeli doctor—this was before the separation wall was constructed—and he responded to Sami with medical help that resulted in their first successful pregnancy. The kindness of near-strangers over a cup of tea resulted in Sami's "quiver now full" of children. His own generous and inclusive spirit opened the door for grace to find him. He showed no partiality when it came to hospitality, and the Spirit seemed similarly inclined.

In the following days, Sami wove us into his neighborhood. His, our, and their stories braided together over cups of fragrant tea. As more chairs materialized, so did more people and more conversations. "Sami loves everyone," neighbors boasted as they popped in for their daily tea. But it was equally clear that everyone loved Sami, both his smile to brighten their day and his tea creating a moment of relief from the heaviness of living behind the separation wall. Advent continues to be illuminated by one ordinary tea vendor embodying hospitality, still an act of resistance in a stingy economy.

I've learned about advent from Luke, but I've seen advent lived by Sami, offering small salvations wherever he can. It's as if in God's economy we are not nearly as powerless or invisible as imperial economies would have us think. In God's economy, salvation includes reconsidering how our economies are structured, who they press upon, and how we can keep our communities safe and sustainable for those visiting from afar and for families, like the holy family.

6

VISIBLE AND INVISIBLE

Shepherds and Angels
Bethlehem | Luke 2:8–21

The story of the first advent, according to Luke's telling, is the story of God pushing boundaries of respectability in pursuit of another kind of peace. An ordinary priest crushed by imperial economics receives an angelic visit amid his service in the temple. A pious, barren woman of later years is with child. A young girl from Galilee, possibly abused and from a region where many women and girls faced bodily trauma, is told by a divine messenger that something is about to change. The Spirit is moving farther and farther from the centers of power and propriety toward those most victimized by the empire. And then God reaches deep into the social fray, stretching all the way to a band of shepherds. The whole of society is embraced by Emmanuel—God with *all* of us, right down to the lowliest shepherd!

Cultural connotations of shepherds at this time and place would have ranged from uncouth to dangerous, from commonplace to undesirable. Elites would have included them in the ranks of the nearly invisible. Shepherds reeked of sheep or goats, of manure and their own sweat. And not in anyone's wildest messianic imaginings would they be expected at the birth of a divine dignitary. Angels maybe, shepherds never. Shepherds were likely kept at arm's length by those of higher status, not accepted except as an economic necessity.

Shepherding was often the work of sons tending their father's flock. Grown men who watched over the family's animals or were hired to manage another man's livestock were low-wage earners and not given much social consideration. To be a shepherd was to do a child's chore your entire life. It was not a path that earned respect; that was reserved for the owners of the herd. The better shepherds knew their sheep and could tell when they were hungry or tired, agitated or sick. The sheep recognized the voice of their shepherd and responded to it. The good shepherds became virtually one with the sheep as they traversed the land together, subjected to the same elements—be it mud or rain or extreme heat. In a fold the shepherd almost blended in with the sheep, hardly noticeable and commanding little regard from anyone other than the loyal animals dependent on them. Shepherding was full of long stretches of tedium and empty time to let one's mind wander with the sheep, to look at the skies, to read the signs of weather, of danger, of the lands that offered grazing to support the flocks.

Shepherds might have been the most emblematic group of Bethlehem. They pointed to the economic realities of the first advent, when the meat industry drove the local economy. They were the "essential workers" of that place and time. Everyday shepherds, though, for all their lowliness, also provoked some of the Judeans' deepest memories, back to the time when Israel was a vibrant kingdom under the rule of one of their own.

David was the favorite son of Bethlehem, the shepherd-boy whom the prophet Samuel recruited from tending his father's sheep in the hills to be anointed as king. His was a rags-to-royalty story shepherds no doubt knew well. It was also the shepherd-king David who composed Psalm 23, singing of green pastures and still waters he likely knew from the gentle slopes of Bethlehem. The contentment of his own flock, well-tended amid the uneven terrain, became an image for human contentment too.

In the system of empires which operate in polarity, shepherds and their kin often lived on the outskirts, thought of as possible troublemakers who didn't quite fit within the system that declared binaries: You were either a citizen of Rome or a supplicant. Either loyal to Caesar or an insurrectionist. Rich or poor. Seen or not seen. In this mentality, shepherds were easily considered enemies of the state or perceived as suspect.

Interesting that in this narrative about how, where, and to whom God arrives, the shepherd is included. It is worth asking what their presence in the first advent says

about God and the peace soon to be announced in Bethlehem. Maybe it points to the extremities of the economy,
where people seldom look. The shepherds of the first
advent might be akin to migrant farm workers of today,
those laboring in fields all around us—nearly unseen and
certainly under-appreciated, yet absolutely essential to
the economy. Invisible, they are the ones most suscepti-
ble to deep exploitation by the systems they serve, which
don't protect them in turn. But they make an appearance
in the first advent—and in every manger scene since—
visible and central in God's vision of peace.

❖ ❖ ❖

Some say the name Bethlehem means "house of bread,"
but more likely it was "house of meat."[1] It was a market
town where animals from the surrounding desert region
were traded, slaughtered, and sold. Sheep also yielded
wool that was spun into yarn and sold for textiles. The
markets were full of animal products of all sorts, including meat, milk, suet, wool, and sheepskin. Merchants,
butchers, and shepherds would have been everywhere.
Bethlehem, for all intents and purposes, was the meat
district of Judea.

Shepherds herded their sheep and goats across the
hills of the region, where the animals could graze, often
without the permission of landowners. Some landowners saw shepherds, and their hungry flocks, as trespassers.
Along with the constant search for vegetation, the herding

included the hunt for water. Obviously, still waters would be the easiest option for shepherd and sheep alike. But in the seasons when the riverbeds dried up, shepherds contended for water from local wells. Their relationship with their neighbors would have been uneven and uneasy, as those who used precious resources. Perhaps their reputation for being contentious, even dangerous, came from these daily skirmishes for local reserves.

The thriving meat economy in Bethlehem connected the city to Jerusalem. Animals from the fields and markets of Bethlehem were sold in the temple courts for sacrifice. Some landowners of the Judean countryside were also priests with a stake in livestock production, profiting off the industry from two segments of the economy.[2] This fact of overlapping, possibly conflicting interests would not have been lost on an ordinary priest like Zechariah, who observed the layers of corruption within the elite priesthood.

❖ ❖ ❖

In the political world of ancient Palestine, other realities also pressed down upon shepherds. Common to all those living on the bottom of the pyramid was the pressure to pay local taxes: both tribute to Rome and tithes to the temple. Failure to pay put individuals in jeopardy of losing what little they had. And for shepherds of low status, there was nowhere else to go but into the clutches of the empire.

Songs of a silent and holy night misunderstand the quiet as calm. It is a signature of privilege to associate peace with a quiet night. For those who live on the edges of the empire, nightfall increases the possibility of danger. Snapping branches, unexpected pops, unidentified rumbling of poachers and natural predators you cannot see through the darkness make for uneasy nights. Trouble can come from any direction. Silence for shepherds is always thick with jeopardy. They know what can be lost before the dawn.

As each day came to a close, shepherds gathered in hushed conversation around a fire at night's edge. They talked of what it had taken to maneuver around the soldiers or avoid the local tax collector for another day while their pockets remained empty. They spoke in vague, oblique terms about the abuse visited upon a sister or a cousin. With a vigilant awareness that words travel even in the dark, they kept their conversations almost inaudible. Harsh words for Caesar's empire and its collaborators were hardly spoken aloud for fear of punishing consequences. Even speaking ill of the empire in discreet company posed a risk.

Nearby was the Herodium fortress, built just outside of Bethlehem. Surrounded by dirt and shaped into a large man-made mountain, the fortress loomed over the landscape as an installation of Herod's surveillance state, allowing him to see all of Bethlehem, as far south as the Dead Sea, across to Jerusalem and Jericho, and all the land in between. This offered reconnaissance for an insecure ruler. And on a micro-level, it housed local informants who listened to words whispered amid busy marketplaces, on crowded streets, and even in the fields. Shepherds knew that nightfall gave no protection from danger.[3]

A legion of soldiers can come upon you at night. They can drag you out and toss you into the troubled darkness. They can take, destroy, or scatter your flocks. They can find your home and family, prey on your daughters while you are away, powerless to help. Or demolish your house, leaving your family instantly displaced. The fear is tangible, and it is made worse after dark. These shepherds, who never made the mistake of equating quiet with peace, minded the sheep and the dark with equal vigilance.[4]

Into this dead of night, angels came. The place of potential trauma would be transformed into a place of stunning revelation for the unexpecting shepherds. And on this night, a new story unfolded against the backdrop of the stiff darkness.

First, one angel came, illuminating the shepherds who wanted to avoid the spotlight. Now they were found, out in the hills and nearly defenseless as Bethlehem slept. The shepherds' instinctive response, conditioned by their landscape, was terror. But the angel interrupted their panic cycle, saying, "Do not fear." This is the language of salvation oracles. Zechariah and Mary had heard these words. Prophets of old heard them, too. When salvation is on the horizon, human fears need to be quelled. Only then can we receive the good news on offer and consider participating in God's salvific work.

The angel continued, saying that the message was one of good news and great joy and intended for *all people*. And on this night, *all people* included the usually unseen shepherds. The word arrived as a birth announcement for a savior. Another savior, a possible rival to Caesar and his peace program across Palestine. This angelic proclamation was political and provocative; it likely alleviated one kind of anxiety but incited another.[5] To speak of a rival ruler was an act of treason. This good news was not uncomplicated or without tension. But for the shepherds, the promise of a peace they could be part of would have been an intriguing proposition.

The angel gave the shepherds a sign of their own—a manger. They would find the savior-child swaddled and lying in a manger. God made the approach familiar for the lowly shepherds. A family that wrapped an infant in swaddling clothes like their own mothers had used would be less frightening; perhaps the parents would be of their own kind. And a place where a child could be cradled in a feeding trough, familiar to them in their line of work, a common dwelling. This might be a special child and a special circumstance, but they could read the sign and anticipate an easy welcome. God's peace initiative entered troubled times and disarmed the fears of those who were often made victims of that trouble.

A newborn found in a feeding trough would not be the expectation for Israel's coming king, but would not necessarily be uncommon in a full house among working-class folks. The manger remains a relic of real life in all its pressing demands and small spaces, where a child is born, just like many other children, into the crush of census season.

While the shepherds absorbed the message and the sign, a host of angels arrived to reinforce the news with shouts of "Glory! Peace!" These angels were not the choir often imagined, but rather warrior voices. Again upending expectations associated with dark nights and the peripheries of towns like Bethlehem, instead of Roman soldiers coming upon the shepherds, an angelic militia arrived. Instead of preying upon the shepherds' fears, the angels' presence bolstered hope. As the holy serenade ended, the angelic host exited. Once again, the night was dark, but it was not without promise.

The shepherds, made silent by the events, now found their voices. They spoke together, made plans to find the child, then began the moonlight search. Once they found the manger, the babe in swaddling clothes, they paid homage to the child. And they spoke with the holy couple, telling of their angelic encounter in the field. When she heard their story, we're told Mary treasured the shepherds' words. Their testimony about their angelic visitation would nourish her for the long, hard days ahead. We will have to wait until Matthew's telling to learn about

Joseph's perspective regarding the birth of his child. But Luke adds one more detail—the shepherds told others the good news. They shared with the townspeople they met along the road about what they'd heard and seen, praising God for the new peace underway.

As for the shepherds, as early prototypes of the disciples and evangelists to come, they were emboldened by being included in God's peace plan. Once invisible, they were chosen to be among the first to witness God's work. No longer would they speak in hushed tones, keep quiet, or stay out of sight. They spoke of what they witnessed to everyone they met as they made their way back to the fields outside of Bethlehem.

❖ ❖ ❖

I first visited the Nassar family and lands just south of Bethlehem in 2017. Like many Palestinian families, they live in a state of uncertainty when it comes to home. Holding on to ancestral land is far from a given, where neighbors regularly experience demolished homes and eviction from family lands and farms.[6] As Jewish settlements grow in the West Bank, Palestinians are displaced. Each family has an increasing sense not only of precarity but of scarcity.

Palestinians have survived many successive regimes: Ottoman, British, Jordanian, and now Israeli. The vexing question of who rightfully owns the land remains. Through the tiers of multiple oppressive legal systems

from the first advent to now, determining ownership
has been fraught, allowing the current government to
bend laws and assert possession of land held for centuries by Palestinian families.[7] Not only does this happen
across the West Bank and in Gaza, but dispossession of
Palestinian property also happens in neighborhoods in
East Jerusalem.[8]

The Nassar family owns a 100-acre farm outside
Bethlehem, land that has been in their legal and well-
documented possession since 1916, when it was pur-
chased by Daher Nassar from the Ottomans.[9] For generations now, the family has farmed olives, almonds,
apricots, grapes, figs, and even wheat on this land. But for
the past thirty years, farming has been met with increasing obstacles, including legal battles around ownership
and harassment from soldiers and settlers alike.

The Nassar land, known as Daher's Vineyard, is
ringed by five Jewish settlements on the surrounding hill-
sides.[10] In the 1970s and '80s, the construction of the settlements worried this Palestinian Christian family. Then
in the 1990s, their farmland, occupying a prime location
atop gently sloping hills, was "redesignated" as Israeli
state land. What followed was the first of many demolition orders the Nassars received.

When I visited with Daoud Nassar, grandson of
Daher, he spoke of the precarious nature of stewarding this land under daily duress. Days before a harvest,
the military came and plowed under their apricot trees.

When the Nassar family rejected a bid on the part of neighboring settlers to build a road through their land, the settlers uprooted 250 of the Nassars' olive trees, hoping to push them to "voluntarily" vacate the land.

For most, this would be fuel for the fire of hatred against these neighbors, causing resistance and violence in a spirit of righteous anger. But guided by the words and witness of Jesus, the Nassar family refuses to be enemies. Instead, when people come to harass them, they offer them tea and a shady place to sit.

When the Nassars' electricity was turned off, they installed solar panels. When they were denied water service, they dug cisterns to catch rainwater. When their trees were uprooted, they planted saplings. The demolition order on their structures meant repurposing caves on the land to shelter the family. In the early years of the Christian church, the apostle Paul wrote a letter to the believers in Rome, still under Roman occupation: Don't repay evil for evil, he wrote. Be at peace with others, and meet evil with good.[11] Even now, as the roads to the Nassar land are barricaded by the military, visitors like us walk across the shallow valley up to the farm and share the hospitality of those living out God's peace amid precarity.

The hallmark of the Nassar family is hospitality. They are an outpost of peace and welcome. The welcome is also a strategy to remain visible in a political climate that seeks to erase and evict them. As they welcome people to their farm, the well-worn footpaths visitors walk lead to conversations about the peacemaking imperative Bethlehem's Child came to teach and about the continuation of the good work and witness of advent's first shepherds. This is a long trajectory of hoped-for peace rooted in Bethlehem, just up the road from the Nassar farm.

◆ ◆ ◆

Advent continues to point to who we see, who we welcome, whose peace we choose to embody. Despite lodging in borrowed quarters, Joseph and Mary received the shepherds, there near the manger. No begging off an unexpected visit from strangers in the night because a child had been born. According to Luke's telling, they made room for the shepherds just as their extended family had made room for them. During times of duress, hospitality among the downtrodden was—and is—a method of mutual survival, and welcome itself added to hope to challenging times.

Advent tells of a regime that rivals that of Caesar, another paradigm for peace whose foundation is justice, not violence. It reminds us there is another way to order the world, where God arrives and Jesus incarnates peace in his life lived among those like him—the poor, the marginalized, the meek.

Stirring up our courage, like the shepherds of that first advent, we share with others the news of a better peace on offer, with its roots in Nazareth and Bethlehem and the Judean hills, where God made visible an alternative way to shape the world.

❖ ❖ ❖

As Luke's advent narrative comes to an end, we recall where his writing comes in history and what he knew about God's peace plan's success. Luke wrote no earlier than 80 CE, long after the crucifixion of Jesus by the state. He wrote after Rome destroyed Jerusalem and the temple in 70 CE. He wrote while Rome still ruled Judea and Galilee. He wrote knowing that God's peace had yet to arrive in its promised fullness.

Like God's kingdom, advent's peace was both now and not yet.

Advent is not immediate. It's a slow peace. God's advent was the start of something profoundly good, a good we still labor to realize today under different regimes, different religions, and different attempts at peace.

We'd like to imagine that when advent dawned, peace came swift and sure to our troubled landscapes. But God's peace comes more like yeast. It develops without hurry, interacting with its environment as it activates and gradually permeates the dough. There is plenty of time to proof the dough, and sometimes multiple rises are necessary to get the dough ready for baking—and eating. This is what peace feels like: something that develops slowly over generations, with our active engagement. It is far from a quick fix. For millennia, across lands and peoples, we continue to be part of that slow, steady salvation inaugurated during the first advent; part of the unfolding hope the angels sang of on the outskirts of Bethlehem that silent and perilous night. Their song has given us hope for all the perilous nights since.

7

GENERATIONS

Joseph

Bethlehem | Matthew 1:18–25

Across the landscape of ancient Palestine—and Matthew's advent narrative—the presence of Herod looms large. If Luke offers us a wide-angle view of Caesar and the Roman Empire as the backdrop for the arrival of Jesus, Matthew zooms in on Herod and the particular menace he posed. The tight focus reveals the more local experience of oppression by Caesar's client-king.

An imperial foil for Matthew, Herod was the face of Rome for Galileans and Judeans. Herod functioned in high contrast to the likes of righteous Joseph, the devout sages from abroad, and the innocent peasants in Bethlehem. It didn't appear to matter that Herod was himself raised as a Jew, married a Maccabean princess, and rebuilt major portions of the Second Temple—his actions and allegiances betrayed him as a man in deference to the empire, more Roman than Jewish.

The young Herod, son of Antipater, a well-connected and savvy political operative in the area, was appointed the governor of Galilee in 47 BCE. He cut his teeth exacting taxes from the restive region and successfully delivering them to Rome.[1] He also rid the terrain of bandits who riddled the roads, going as far as commanding that they be killed without trial.[2] This kind of track record quickly won him favor with the imperial powers, who cared little about his brutal tactics. In that respect, he seemed cut from their cloth.

Next, the Roman Senate appointed him "King of the Jews." This made him sole ruler of the region. He worked to defeat the remaining vestiges of the Maccabean family, thus firmly establishing the Herodian dynasty and a heavy, cruel reign that lasted thirty-seven years.

During his tenure, he increased militarism in the form of secret police reporting on the population; additional forces were tasked with containing protestors and other kinds of troublemakers. His personal militia of thousands gave him extra protection from the masses. So disliked and distrusted by the people was he that his insecurity was warranted.

Another source of Herod's insecurity was Antony and Cleopatra. He owed Antony his position as King of Judea, so his fortunes rose and fell along with Antony's amid the civil war afoot in the empire. Simultaneously, Herod was unnerved by Cleopatra, who had her own designs on Judea and the surrounding regions. Antony gifted her some of Herod's territory, and Herod felt her hot breath on the back of his neck.[3]

Herod's own mother-in-law, Alexandra, attempted to conspire with Cleopatra to gain a political win over her son. And a continuing skirmish with Maccabean hold-outs disloyal to him kept him on edge. The political insecurity that fueled Herod on these multiple fronts further endangered those he ruled. Insecure and tyrannical leaders were part of the first advent—and have been part of most Advents since.

As Luke gave us a window into the advent economy and environment, Matthew shows us what that economy looked like through an understanding of one person's rule: that of Herod. The economy he presided over was one of heavy taxation for the masses, funding the tribute to Rome as well as Herod's own lavish building projects across the region. During his tenure, Herod built palaces for himself and his family. He built stadiums, theatres, even entire cities for Caesar. And he constructed many fortresses, including the infamous Masada[4] and Herodium, that mountain-shaped complex on the edge of Bethlehem that set the shepherds on edge and allowed Herod eyes over the expanse of Roman Palestine.

But the elaborate expansion of the temple complex was Herod's most ambitious undertaking—and the one he hoped would win over the support of his Jewish kin. He extended the outer courtyards, added chambers and halls, and embellished every corner of the temple complex with architectural flourish. The completed renovation was glorious, but insufficient in wooing the populace or convincing them that he was truly Jewish. While his building prowess curried favor with Rome, it never won over the people of Galilee or Judea. Herod's heart seemed to hunger for an acceptance that even Rome's title could not offer him—the affection of the people was not for the empire to give. In the first advent, we begin to see fissures in the imperial structures and the insecurities of the rulers, despite their military might.

And each of Herod's new endeavors came at a cost to the people. The increased tax burden weighed on families and pushed people to take risk-laden loans in last-ditch efforts to hold on to ancestral land. But the risk often resulted in more loss—enslavement, tenant farming, or confiscated land.

In addition to the militarized atmosphere and increased taxes, there was Herod's legendary cruelty. He quelled an early threat to his throne by his charismatic relative and rival, Aristobulus III, arranging for the popular Maccabean prince to be drowned.[5] He also ordered the killing of his own wife, brother-in-law, and three sons over the course of his life. Even in the courts of Caesar, Herod was considered vicious for his treatment of family—and anyone else who got in his way.

This was the atmosphere of advent in Matthew's Gospel.

In bringing Herod to the fore, with the title King of the Jews conferred on him by Caesar but with no Jewish expectation attached to his name, Matthew displays the power structure that would greet the forthcoming holy child. Yet he builds the child's own genealogy in the beginning of his gospel narrative in such a way as to point to another structure in operation. With ancestral connection to Abraham, Isaac, and Jacob, as well as to Jesse and his son, King David, the biological trajectory was set for Messiah. Jesus would enter the Judean landscape that was aligned with Jewish hopes, even as his birth in Bethlehem carried the prophetic narrative of the coming Messiah forward.

Matthew offers a final summary to his genealogy, a repeating heptad of names. There were fourteen generations between Father Abraham and King David, another fourteen generations between King David and the deportation of Jews to Babylon, and another fourteen generations from the Babylonian captivity to the arrival of the Christ child—a total of six sets of seven. In Hebraic literature, the number seven signified perfection, completion, or maturity.

The placement of Jesus at the head of the seventh heptad signaled to Matthew's Jewish audience the significance of the subject of this genealogy. As the first name of the final set of seven, Jesus inaugurated the beginning of a new humanity, a new experience of peace, a new kind of kingdom coming. The next six names in the final cycle would be those who continued God's campaign into the future. Jesus would not be the last. From advent on, those adopted into God's family are descendants in this genealogy, invited to join this story of a new humanity living differently in troubled times.[6] In the genealogy of those who follow Jesus, the peace campaign continues. For those of us in this family, we are the heirs of the first advent.

In contrast, Herod's family line was rumored to have come through Babylon,[7] perhaps grown in the soil of exile and then of Idumea, where some Jewish families had moved upon their return from captivity. The merit of this story was that it lent credibility to Herod's undocumented history amid a sea of Jewish families with meticulous genealogical records. Maybe Herodian family archives had gotten lost in the fog of captivity, diaspora, and repatriation—at least that's one theory of the case. Still, most Jews doubted Herod's true Jewishness; it was a battle he could never win in his homeland.

Perhaps even Matthew was needling Herod in retrospect with the oblique mention of those who did go to and return from Babylon. But what we know is that Jesus's ancestors came through exile and that Jesus began something bona fide and new. According to Matthew, Jesus's lineage is uncontested, pointing to him as the rightful King of the Jews—something that would become clear in time.[8] This is the story of his beginning, already more credentialed than Herod's. And it is only the first of many ways Jesus will be seen in high contrast to Herod and his cruel, self-aggrandizing, insecure ways.

With the root system of Jesus's family tree and the distinctions between him and Herod made clear, Matthew turns our attention to the birth of God's child in Bethlehem—the first advent presenting a rival practitioner of a different sort of peace. We will also now see the advent narrative from a different vantage point: from that of Joseph, Mary's betrothed.

❖ ❖ ❖

In my theological studies and early readings of the advent narratives, I was taught that the birth of Jesus announced by the angels meant peace had at last landed on earth. No one noted what seems clear to me now: advent speaks to the arrival of God's peace initiative, the *beginning* of the campaign. There's a perpetual call to embody peace in our troubled times. And I see advent as both a call and an ongoing answer, because peace is never fully realized this side of eternity.

Jesus brought the beginning of peace. And those who follow his lead work for the fulfilment of it. Jesus showed us what living at peace could look like—how to respond to the places, people, and politics around us. Along with the gifts of advent, his life bequeathed to us the challenge to make choices in keeping with peace, wherever we are embedded in the world. As I, as we, live into the reality of advent hope, we embody God's peace, not only in struggle, lament, and solidarity with others but also in the shared experience of patience for the unhurried culmination of a peaceable kingdom. The life of a peacemaker embraces the hard truth that peace will remain incomplete in our lifetime, even as others carry the campaign forward. This was the human experience of Jesus.

The tenure of Jesus's ministry brimmed with peacemaking choices and even moments of calmed storms, healed bodies, restored minds, and the offering of unexpected meals for the hungry. Yet when Jesus spoke of economic justice, as he often did, his life was threatened, as when he nearly got pushed off a cliff.[9] When he worked liberative goodness and returned people to community life, he was held in suspicion for his timing. When he set people free from possession—psychological traumas likely caused by colonization—he was accused of consorting with the devil. And when Jesus preached the good news of a nonviolent kingdom, his theological credentials were questioned.[10] The practice of peace did not bring acceptance from all. And eventually, committing his life to peacemaking put him in direct conflict with the powers of the day, ending with the state executing him as a terrorist.

"He thought he was the King of the Jews," they mocked as they watched him die in the heat of the day. Jesus had embodied another way of living under the imperial occupation of Rome, and it got him killed. He never saw the culmination of peace and the fullness of justice dawn during the span of his human lifetime. For all his peace and patience, he collapsed into God, whom he trusted to continue the peace initiative even in his earthly absence.

And this is where we come in, we who follow the call of subsequent advents. We carry on God's mission of peace in the world, under the empires and colonial dynamics of our day. Jesus, raised from the dead, imparts the Spirit to guide this ongoing peacemaking campaign from one generation to the next. Even knowing that peace likely won't arrive on our horizon, still we advance the advent imperative, living at peace with others, equipping the next generation of peacemakers.

❖ ❖ ❖

Matthew set the scene with his genealogy, prophecy, and Herodian context. Now he directs our attention to the birth of Jesus, recounted in his own words. Mary and Joseph, her betrothed, are finally named in the narrative. And Matthew moves to the heart of the advent story with a radically different vantage point than that of Luke. Where Luke focused on the girl from Galilee, Matthew now focuses on Joseph. The narrative presents Joseph as a just man. We should understand him as such, amid an unjust empire. But soon Matthew shows that the deck is stacked against Joseph and his young bride.

We often think of justice as having to do with obeying laws, the meting out of punishment, matters of civil rights, and so forth. But in Scripture, most often it is about *economic justice*. It is about equitable distribution and returning things (land, labor, livestock, etc.) to their rightful owners.[11] In the context of the advent scene that Matthew unfolds, we meet again with Mary, who would have returned now from visiting Elizabeth, and whose pregnancy has started to show. Joseph, the just man, decides that he will not compound her trouble with a messy divorce; he'll be quiet about it. So we get a glimpse into the depth of Joseph's character and commitment to a just life in his response to Mary and the situation precipitated by her untimely pregnancy.

The couple were betrothed, which was a legally binding part of the ancient marriage arrangement and occurred before the home-going to the husband's family and home. Breaking off the marriage at this point involved matters of law (hence the language of divorce), showing it to be unlike the ending of a modern engagement. A man in Joseph's position could ask for economic compensation in addition to the divorce—the impounding of the dowry and possible return of the bride price.[12] But that would require public conversations with Joseph's community elders and would make known Mary's compromised condition. She was already on the verge of public disgrace, but she still mattered to him. A quiet divorce, he decided, would avoid compounding her shame, even if it meant forfeiture of his dowry. It was not worth the monetary benefit to push someone lower, and Mary was already down, as far as Joseph's calculations were concerned. Likely, he would have to endure social scorn if he did not clear his name publicly in divorce proceedings.[13] Still, he seemed willing to accept a measure of shared shame to shield her from society's worst.

In Joseph, a different economic practice was at work. He valued Mary as a person, beyond what sum of money he could demand.

I think Joseph showed himself to value a different economic practice than did his namesake, the patriarch Joseph in the book of Genesis, who participated in Egypt's economy of empire with different values at play. This may not be an echo from the Hebrew Bible that Matthew intended, but I cannot ignore the juxtaposition of these two men. When appointed as food czar by Pharaoh, Joseph engaged in imperial economics according to Egypt's rules, in which he made Pharaoh richer and the peasantry poorer. Joseph's complicity in the economic system of the empire also contributed to the enslavement of many, including his kin.[14] And by the time he realized his mistake, it was too late.

The first Joseph cried out on his deathbed, asking that his bones be carried out of Egypt with his Hebrew people when they finally experienced liberation, since that would now be the only way he could share in their freedom. While he was considered a pious man, it did not surface in his work as an economic practitioner. His economic imagination kept him loyal to Pharaoh and kept him from enacting emancipation on behalf of his own people. The scene haunts me—the patriarch unable to participate in deliverance.

But Joseph the Just was altogether different. His mind was set on valuing Mary and facilitating a future with less stigma, rather than on the money of empire. He would be a different sort of patriarch, fathering a new economic calculus for those on the road of God's liberating peace.

He tried to sleep. But a dream disrupted his slumber. Into the darkness, an angel appeared. And by this time in the advent story, no one is surprised that the first words spoken to Joseph were "Do not fear." What came next, though, was another reversal: "Do not divorce Mary," the messenger said. God's own child was coming through her to bring salvation into the world.

Joseph obeyed the angel. In doing so, he said yes to Mary, to her child, and to the stigma of the situation. He awoke to the harsh reality that he'd be implicated by her too-early pregnancy.

Even before the angel spoke, Joseph had put Mary first, not the money that society said he should expect. He had evolved beyond his namesake, prioritizing differently even amid a hard economy in which every shekel counted. And after the angel spoke to him in the dream, Joseph proved to be both pious and a just economic practitioner, as he refrained from intimate relations with Mary until after the Spirit-breathed child was born. He was, indeed, a just man in more ways than one.

Once again, we see how economics intersect with the first advent. In Joseph's case, it was not about charity as he awaited the birth of this special child; it was the willingness to forgo economic compensation that he could have rightly claimed, for the sake of the well-being of another.

So Joseph and Mary limped their way through the betrothal. He entered into her disgrace. Now the questions that surrounded them were about *their* piety and purity. They shouldered the shame together. The men at the city gate likely demeaned Joseph, no longer thinking him righteous. But God had invited him into the heart of the divine deliverance operation—along with its social stigma. Indeed, following the unborn Christ already had consequences.

When Mary gave birth to Jesus, Joseph named him as his son in obedience to the angel's instruction. This was an adoption, a public recognition that the child was his and would carry his name into the world. It showed, as Matthew intended, that Joseph accepted Mary into his cherished lineage—and Jesus too.

The first advent revealed that leaning into God's coming justice puts people at odds with society's and religion's definitions of holiness. Advent just might make life harder. Yet we know what Joseph knew: God is with us. This is how Matthew sets up the story. Joseph and Mary held fast to the assurance of God-with-us. Soon the story would unfold in God being with them physically—in their very arms.

According to Matthew's narrative, the holy couple resided in Bethlehem. Surrounded by family and midwives in their own modest home, Mary gave birth to Jesus. Maybe Elizabeth even traveled from Ein Kerem to assist in the delivery and support her highly revered relative. But Matthew pulls away from details of the birth story of Jesus. He returns to the overall origin story he has begun to develop. And soon enough, readers of his Gospel see Herod's reaction to a rival king.[15]

❖ ❖ ❖

In the book of Isaiah, the prophet tells King Ahaz: "Look, the young woman is with child and shall bear a son, and shall name him Immanuel. . . . For before the child knows how to refuse the evil and choose the good, the land before whose two kings you are in dread will be deserted."[16]

The name Immanuel—meaning "God is with us"—was given as an assurance during politically perilous times. Ahaz, Judah's king, floundered in panic as two neighboring countries sought to oust him from leadership and invade the southern kingdom. But the prophet Isaiah told him to "stand firm in faith."[17] Even as the king continued to cower, God volunteered a sign for the anxious king, at first asking Ahaz what sign he might seek. When Ahaz refused to answer, still God gave the king a sign of assurance, that he would survive this looming threat if he opted for faith over fear, and Isaiah spoke the prophecy of Immanuel.

According to the story Isaiah told, a pregnant woman was ready to give birth; from the sound of things, the baby might even be crowning. That her son would be named Immanuel was a sign that God was at work in the present situation. And before the child could grow to tell right from wrong (so, before he turned two years old), the entire conflict with the hostile kings would be over. God gave the sign in order to incubate faith in King Ahaz as he waited out the military menace poised on his borders.

Hundreds of years later, Matthew wrote down the good news of Jesus. Times were still hard. Rome had destroyed Jerusalem, and infighting riddled the young movement of Jesus-followers.[18] Matthew encouraged the congregation to hold fast and keep faith in Jesus even as trials beset them. And the Gospel writer began by telling the story of Jesus's birth. In the process, he quotes Isaiah—saying that this child will be called Immanuel. Those who knew the story of King Ahaz would surely recognize the name. It spoke of God's presence and hinted that once again they stood on a precipice between faith and fear in the midst of perilous political times.[19]

In Matthew's origin story about Jesus, as Joseph decides to end the betrothal quietly and not terrorize Mary further, the angel who visits him whispers that name that has come down through time—*Emmanuel*. And with that name comes an understanding of the ancient prophecy: a young woman, pregnant, soon to birth a son.

Some thirty-three years later, as Jesus stands among his disciples on a Galilean mountaintop one last time, he will say to them, "Remember, *I am with you* always, to the end of the age."[20] The echo of the name will not be missed. No matter what his frightened friends and followers would meet in the future—the post-crucifixion chaos, the loss and confusion, the rumors of a resurrection—he would be with them to the end of the age, for all the time they could imagine. And so they choose faith in the God present with them through Jesus—Emmanuel—once again and always.

While King Ahaz allowed fear to win the day, Joseph awoke to greater faith. And as Matthew wrote to his congregation about the advent story, he reminded them of Emmanuel—God with them—a signature of advent urging all of us to hold on to the presence of God despite troubled times, despite fear.

❖ ❖ ❖

Matthew made it clear in his advent narrative that a new liberation story was afoot. Even in the composition of a genealogy, he made choices that spoke of liberation, such as stating that Joseph's father's name was Jacob.[21] It was a nod to the Jacob and Joseph of Genesis, and to Israel's origin story. It triggered memories about the Hebrews once enslaved in Egypt, where the Jewish liberation story was birthed under Pharaoh's empire, not unlike the empire the people were currently living under. Maybe Matthew was hinting at something new happening, like a new exodus.

The thread of the exodus story continued in Matthew's Gospel, as he wrote about Joseph's on, off, and then on-again relationship with Mary. In the telling is an echo of a story in the Talmud about Amram, who would become the father of Moses. Upon learning of Pharaoh's death decree for baby boys, Amram decided to divorce his wife to prevent the birth of future children.[22] He would not give Pharaoh more Hebrews to kill. But through his young daughter, a revelation came. Miriam instructed her father to reunite with his wife. So he remarried her, and soon they conceived a son—Moses. Marked for death by Pharoah, Moses became the deliverer of the Hebrew people even as he dismantled Pharaoh's regime.

The pattern of divorce, revelation, and remarriage is one Matthew wove into his gospel, revealing Jesus as the new Moses, one who would bring a new exodus for the Jewish people living under Rome,[23] and economic emancipation for those trying to survive Herod's oppressive rule.[24] In Matthew's advent narrative, this would not be the last echo of the exodus.

❖ ❖ ❖

Walking down the cobblestone alley from Star Street, where I had left off from Chef Fadi's inn and Sami's tea kiosk, I continued to Manger Square. Standing there, I inhaled the aroma of fresh-roasted nuts, falafel, and the air of Bethlehem, heavy with history: the place where Joseph and Mary lived, shopped at the open-air markets, visited with neighbors in these streets. Somewhere not too far from where I walked, Mary's water broke, her son crowned, and the family celebrated the arrival of the next generation.

I continued walking, off the shoulder of Manger Square to the Milk Grotto, where, legend has it, Mary spilled some breast milk. The small, rounded spaces filled with images of a breastfeeding mother reminded me of Mary's early days of motherhood. This was the place of the first latch, the first hungry cry, the first of many sleepless nights for the new parents. As I walked in Bethlehem, each young family passing on the road breathed life into the humanity of advent's first family. This was where they began to embody advent newness.

Not too far in another direction, at a corner of Manger Square, sits the Church of the Nativity. I wandered in. And as I always do when there, I lit a candle before Mother Mary. I made the sign of the cross, acknowledging the visit. "Hail, Mary, full of grace!" I exhaled, like cousin Elizabeth greeting my Lord's blessed mother.

I slid into one of the wooden pews, smooth from all the pilgrims before me. I wondered why I keep returning to this place. The Spirit whispered, "This land matters. Incarnation happened here. Pay attention." These words, that singular moment, drew me to the advent narrative and began my own season of reflection on God's peace and this place.

What did it mean for Jesus to be shaped by this landscape, this economy, this political environment? To be born into anxious times and surrounded by family eking out a living under Roman occupation? How did that form his imagination? After his mother's milk ceased, did he suffer from malnourishment like many other neighborhood children? Did he overhear conversations riddled with fears of losing homes or jobs? Were his uncles detained by soldiers—Roman or Herodian? Did his dark skin, Galilean accent, and Jewish mannerisms make him a target for ridicule or incessant suspicion by the elites?

That God was incarnated in this time and this place matters, I thought. This landscape was formative for Jesus and for God's peace initiative. Now, sitting in the town of his birth, I began to take in with renewed seriousness an awareness that these streets had shaped his earthly experience and continue to instruct pilgrims about the origin story of the advent child.

This land, I said to myself, was marked by incarnation. The indelible impression lingers all these generations later, as pilgrims come to honor the Holy Family and the place where God's peace initiative began to unfold.

The first advent recorded in history and held in our collective Christian memory is not a singular event, a once-and-for-all peace. Advent is continually embodied, incessantly incarnated. Advent reaches across the generations, always pushing us to embody God's peace in today's troubled times. We recognize the signature of advent not in Herod but in the true king, Jesus. Generations brought us to the first advent in Bethlehem, as Matthew demonstrates. And generations will keep advent and seek advent's promise of peace in seasons to come.

8

UNEXPECTED HOPE

Herod, Magi, and a Star
Bethlehem | Matthew 2:1–12

Travel from Jerusalem to Bethlehem requires you to cross a checkpoint to pass through the separation wall between Israel and Palestine's West Bank. The first time I approached the checkpoint, I was in a tour bus with women from different backgrounds and various strands of the Christian tradition, eager to meet peacemakers in the region. Crossing into occupied territory usually means your bus is boarded by Israeli soldiers, rifles in hand—not what most expect on a journey to Bethlehem. For the women on the tour, it signaled that we were entering fraught space—that the West Bank, and whatever lay behind the separation wall, was dangerous.

But just past the checkpoint there unfolded a landscape familiar to me: inviting scenes of shops with goods stacked high and pouring out onto the street, some with fruit stands, others with legs of lamb or beef hanging from hooks. People bobbed and weaved around the displayed inventory and friendly shopkeepers. Men sat out front of shops, playing games. Women surveyed produce and chatted. The streets brimmed with life, not unlike the East African streets I was accustomed to back home. As we drove along these narrow roads, I felt my shoulders drop and my breathing slow. There was nothing more to fear in Bethlehem than in my hometown or in any number of cities I've visited, where life brims even amid political strife.

Still, there was little doubt we'd crossed over into another kind of terrain: the red warning signs, bullet-holed walls, and uneven roads told the story of an occupied land, a less-resourced place.

On a subsequent visit, when I returned with Claude, our taxi driver, Naïef, offered to show us the Banksy graffiti painted across Bethlehem, starting with the well-known wall art of a man throwing not the Molotov cocktail you might expect, but a bouquet of flowers.[1] I'd seen the work cropped on postcards, so the surprise of seeing it at least ten feet tall on the side of a petrol station was awe-inspiring. It remains an iconic image of nonviolent resistance. Then Naïef took us to see smaller works across the city, including one of Mother Mary tossing hearts on a nondescript cinder wall, as well as the symbol of a dove in a flak jacket carrying an olive branch at the center of a busy intersection[2]—each one an artistic missive scribbling a message of hope against the hard gray of occupation.

After we saw the Banksy flower piece, our new friend took us to the Walled Off Hotel to view more artwork by the artist.[3] At the hotel, we shared tea in bone china cups on a lovely patio an arm's length from the separation wall, the dissonance purposeful and clear. Naïef told us what life was like growing up in Bethlehem before the wall. As he watched its construction cutting through Hebron Street, he became aware of the immediate and long-term separation that would prevent his family from visiting Jerusalem from that time on. We mused in hope about a day when the wall would come down, like the Berlin Wall had, and he could visit Jerusalem again.

Next, Naïef drove us to Shepherds' Field, the place he believes Jesus was born. And for the best look at Bethlehem, he drove us up to Herodium. He raved about the view, which, of course, was Herod's point. An ancient surveillance state required such a panoramic perspective of the population to track their movements and antici-pate any resistance.

Despite all Herod's surveillance efforts, though, he never did see the star.

In his advent narrative, Matthew describes that bright star appearing, pointing to a promise for all occu-pied lands from west to east, ancient and contemporary. And those in this account who come from the East, from another land and religious tradition—the magi—are the ones who crack open our understanding about hope in hard places, about resistance, and about the necessity of stars.

Occupied territories like Bethlehem bristle with tension. The air is thick with the fragrance of oranges and olives, but also with the political dynamics that burden residents and put perceptive visitors in a state of constant vigilance. But even amid these troubled communities, tangible signs of hope are found, energizing resistance and subversive action.

When pilgrims travel, as the magi did, from faraway places in a spirit of solidarity, hungry for an infusion of hope to bring back to their own hard landscape, Matthew's narrative comes alive with the fraught political climate that nonetheless hosts hope, not only for its inhabitants, but for the wise wayfarers from the East.

◆ ◆ ◆

For centuries, opposition to Hellenization had reached beyond the West into the eastern regions. When Alexander the Great defeated the Persians in 330 BCE, he brought the influences of the West to their world. Even as subsequent generations longed for a return to indigenous culture and Persian leadership, the discontent did not materialize into a peasant movement against Greek economic exploitation, as it did in Palestine. Still, many elites, like the magi, carried within themselves a spirit of resistance to the Hellenization of their land.[4]

Like many in the ancient Near East, Persians believed that kings were connected to divinity. To claim a foreign king was to dethrone not merely their own political leader but their god. Many people held a deep desire to return to rulers who would respect their Persian kin and ways—and their god.

This is the landscape the magi traveled, navigating peril and promise. As sages who stewarded wisdom as well as other kinds of local and civic knowledge, magi had access to power in cultivating resistance traditions in Persian lands. They pushed against the Hellenization of their culture and religion, working for a future restoration.[5] And a rising star in the sky gave them reason to believe regime change was possible. They were even willing to go westward, like Abraham of Ur, to a place they did not know—a move likely rooted in resistance. Perhaps in the sign of an indigenous king to be restored to the Judean throne, they recognized a hope not unlike their own for a restored Persian ruler. The magi discerned the possibility of hope.

The magi followed with openness and hunger, unaware of where the star would ultimately lead. Going toward the west, toward enemy territory, took courage. Against the headwinds of the ruling regime in Persia and generations of subjugation, they slipped away to find and honor another ruler. When the star took them to Herod's doorstep, they entered undaunted. We will soon learn that they resisted collaborating with that ruler too.

Then, following the star again, they came to a small village in Judea, an outpost of Rome's empire. There they found the young king. They honored him, recognizing his authority. They presented gifts, including Persian gold, known to be a prized commodity in the ancient Near East and internationally.[6] That the magi traveled to find a new king, carrying gold along with them, points to the political freight of their mission. Their travel, their gifts, their homage to the Bethlehemite king pointed to possible treason. But they weren't looking in Judea for a king for themselves, just perhaps for one who could thwart the Hellenizing overlords of the West and so bolster their hope: for if it could happen in Judea, it could happen in Persia.

They found the king in a most unexpected place. The elite functionaries must have been surprised that the star guided them to such an ordinary, even lowly family. But they believed this child was the origin of a new regime that might also signal their future freedom. And they worshipped him.

Herod had requested that they return with news. Instead, they went home another way, taking with them another treason-worthy gift: new hope.

As the original superpower of the ancient Near East, Persia had been expansive and wealthy.[7] After defeat by Alexander the Great, Persians, and the magi as their priestly and political connective tissue, harbored deep memories of their once-dominant kingdom.

Some of the people welcomed the Greek imperial influence even as it unraveled local culture and religions. Others saw resistance as futile, so they accepted Hellenistic ways. But the magi held on to traditions and their national identity. What did they have but stories, wisdom, relationships, and occasional access to elite leaders? Without a Persian king, their influence had waned. However, their skills, connections, and continued proximity to informal power brokers allowed them to build a small measure of clandestine subversion. The magi kept stories alive and propagated prophecies in and beyond Persian lands. And it was their resistance work in their own homeland that brought them to this intersection with the Holy Family.

❖ ❖ ❖

For the people of Persia, peace and local rule were not durable. Cyrus the Great had inaugurated his own grand peace—perhaps the first that Persians had known—in 550 BCE. His reign over Persia, from Central Asia to Mesopotamia and stretching as far as Egypt, has been called the Pax Persica for the time of relative peace across the lands he ruled.[8] The peace lasted about two hundred years, ending with the arrival of Alexander the Great from Macedonia. Whether the peaceful rule was delivered by Cyrus or Caesar, or the short-lived season of self-rule by the Maccabees, the militaristic and economic violence wrought by empires never delivered liberation for all. What remained was the longing for a lasting peace without imperial oppression.

As the Persians yearned for peace, so did the people of Roman Palestine. And God excluded neither from the signs and wonders of the first advent. Centuries after the end of the Persian peace, a star rose in the east. It rose in the aftermath of Persia's days as the first superpower and rose over the ashes of their cities burned and temples pillaged by Macedonia. The star appeared as the magi were likely on the cusp of giving up hope that Persian culture and faith could be saved. Yet they kept looking at the skies and retelling the prophecies of an indigenous leader coming to the throne again. When that star rose, so did their hopes.

Some ancients thought of stars as celestial beings. And some call magi astrologers, minders of the stars. So the connection of stars and magi in Matthew's narrative seems natural. Outside forces, in the sky and in the East, conspired to participate in the advent of God on earth.

❖ ❖ ❖

Matthew's Gospel announces the birth of Jesus in Bethlehem as happening during the reign of Herod, the same ruler whose cadre of advisors missed the birth announcement in the sky. Perhaps building projects and maintaining the status quo had distracted them.

But when that star rose, sages from the East set off from Persia hungry for hope. They believed, like most at that time, that the star likely indicated the birth of a significant person—a ruler, perhaps. Maybe as they followed it, moving toward the west, then toward Judea, then homing in on the city of Jerusalem, where they met Herod, they began to discern that the king they sought was the King of the Jews. Perhaps they were familiar with Jewish prophecies and saw them as coinciding with their hopes for liberation in their own homeland.

Entry through the city gates of Jerusalem must have made clear that this was very much Herod's world. As foreign dignitaries of sorts, they presented themselves at the palace, where they could expect to be received by the ruler. Magi were not mere religious sages. They were men of stature, conversant with and perceptive about the machinations of empires and transitions of power. When magi spoke, people listened—because thrones might be at stake.

"Where is the new King of the Jews?" the magi asked Herod, the current king of the Jews. Unnerved by the question of a rival king, especially coming from visitors outside his realm, Herod leaned in and listened. "We saw his star and have come to worship him"—*worship* being the familiar expression for showing homage to a political superior.[9] That they reserved their tribute for the new king, not Herod, would have troubled him further, since he had known nothing to that point of a potential usurper. Eager to know the true nature and location of the threat to his throne, he asked what else they knew about this king. This was not an innocent inquiry about his successor, but a plot emerging on the spot to protect his power by removing anyone who stood in his way, as he had done with his brother-in-law, Aristobulus III.[10]

Herod brought in his scribes and priests to ask them where this king was to be born. *Where* was the operative word. Where—so the magi could worship. Where—so Herod could eliminate the threat. The advisors told him of the prophecy of Micah, that a child was to be born in Bethlehem of Judea.[11] The outsiders may have known the time, but the insiders knew the place.

Herod passed that information on to the magi, even as he inquired further about the star and calculated his next move. He instructed the sages to report back, ostensibly so he could join them in honoring the new king.

After the magi took their leave, Herod gathered his circle of advisors, men both religious and political who benefited from Herod's tenure. All felt threatened—or, as Matthew tells it, frightened—by the news. *Frightened,* similar to how Zechariah and Mary had been troubled by Gabriel's sudden appearance. But here the fear is not a well-placed response to God's messenger, but the fear associated with a looming loss of privilege. A new king would mean reconsidering current loyalties and recalibrating allegiances, an upending of established economic arrangements.

The magi left Jerusalem, but they didn't need to rely on the words of Herod's advisors, as the very star they had followed from the East reappeared. Once again, they rejoiced at the celestial guide, which now led them to the small town of Bethlehem. The star aligned over the house where Joseph and Mary were living with their son. Even the cosmos conspired to reveal the political winds changing with the advent of the new king.

❖ ❖ ❖

When we went to Banksy's Walled Off Hotel, I ventured upstairs to the gallery and viewed the collection of Palestinian art housed on site. There, for the first time, I encountered the work of Sliman Mansour. He offers a visual connection to aspects of Palestinian culture in ways that open up ideas, rather than reducing them to tropes.

Mansour entered the world in a small town just north of Ramallah, a year before the State of Israel was formed. When he was barely four years old, his father's death necessitated Mansour's and his mother's move to Jerusalem. When he was older, he moved just south to Bethlehem, where he attended the Evangelical Lutheran School. But what he remembers vividly—and what shows up in his paintings in the work of cultural memory-keeping—are the days spent with his grandmother in the Palestinian countryside. With only basic materials at hand, beginning with the mud she formed from the land, she made beehives and chicken coops. No wonder those memories lived on in Mansour's imagination for years to come. In his visits he also listened to his grandfather speak of his love for Palestinian literature and folklore, words and ideas that saturated the young boy's mind. In Mansour's earliest years the influences of place, soil, and story began to shape his understanding and impact his artmaking.

Before Mansour could board a plane to realize his dream of attending the Chicago Art Institute, the Six-Day War broke out. Life as he knew it ended.[12] It was in the heart of occupied Jerusalem that he was forced to continue his art education. Instead of the opportunity to flee subjugated space, he now learned to navigate it and even create new works in a place of tension.

During the occupation of his homeland, the place of his family history and creativity, Mansour discovered an unexpected element emerging for his artwork as Palestine became, as he said in an interview, a land "full of contradiction and full of problems."[13] When, in the 1960s and '70s, the Israeli administration isolated artists from one another and from the international arts community, Mansour deepened his work with the politics of place and local culture, infusing it with resistance. Even as the government confiscated art and restricted artists' movements within Palestine, his artistic sensibilities became more fully shaped through the land, the people, the literature, the call for justice, and the mud.

At one point, as Mansour tells it, he was taken to police headquarters and questioned. Asked why he created political art—art that depicted the artifacts of Palestinian life like olive trees, villages, people in traditional dress, and Jerusalem—he listened as an officer "suggested" to him, "Why not just paint pretty flowers? Even I would buy one of your paintings." But that did not suit Mansour. The officer made it clear that artists like him were not even allowed to use the colors of their flag (black, red, green, and white) in any of their artwork. "How can we paint a watermelon, then?" one fellow artist asked. "You can't," came the response.[14]

Upon learning of this exchange, Palestinian artists began painting watermelons as a symbol of resistance to the occupation. And Mansour continued creating images that reflected the reality he remembered from the past and experienced in the present.

I stood in front of Mansour's canvases in the gallery and saw the Palestinian land awash in color, telling the story of a good life that was, and that could be again on the other side of occupation. Terraced olive groves, a favorite theme, manifested a familiar feature of the landscape I'd come to love. Each brushstroke revealed a connection to this tree, tended with fidelity by families from generation to generation. The presence of the olive tree in Mansour's works told of the fruit's necessity, its durability, even its refusal to fade away under decades of hardship. It resonated with the life I witnessed as I traveled the West Bank—abundant orchards, bowls piled with olives on the breakfast table, golden olive oil flooding plates of fresh labneh and za'atar. The olive trees spoke of life despite hardship.

One recent painting showed a terraced grove torn asunder, trees inverted and set aflame with burnished hues. This, Mansour seems to say, is how the land feels now. Yet the trees remain even in their distress connected to the land as a perpetual symbol of resistance. There remains a stubborn hope, even as the orchards burn. In Mansour's work I see another route home, much like in the story of the magi. This work is a way to tell hard truths about life and loss. It creates room for lament, but also hope for a future shaped by Advent's peace, where trauma can be transformed and goodness reclaimed by those who have never stopped loving and stewarding their homeland.

As the conflict between occupation and Palestinian artists intensified in the decades following the Six-Day War, artists like Mansour were emboldened to create fresh work reflecting the truth of their life in the West Bank and East Jerusalem. They created prints for posters and wider distribution. They created smaller works of art that could be smuggled in cars, circulated from place to place to avoid the inevitable confiscation.[15]

More than once in this season Mansour was put in prison by Israeli officers for incitement.[16] Studio 74, his art gallery in Ramallah, was shut down and all artwork on display confiscated four hours into a new exhibit. Still, he created. Still, he told the truth of his history.

Then the Intifada broke out across the West Bank in 1987, a resistance movement sprouting from the anguish of the Palestinian people.[17] They boycotted Israeli goods. Mansour and his colleagues[18] eschewed Israeli art supplies and opted for indigenous materials like wood, leather, henna, found objects, and mud as a sign of both solidarity and resistance.

Mansour transformed the mud of his youth into material that reflected the cracked reality of life under occupation. His artwork became known around the globe.

"The life you live here forces you to deal with these problems, and little by little, you find yourself a political artist," Mansour said about his evolution into that role. "It was not a decision I made," he added. But his art gives Palestinian people everywhere "a home, homeland, and future."[19]

Whether seen in the West Bank or the diaspora, Mansour's art shines like the star over a humble home in Bethlehem, hope in the dark of troubled landscapes the world over. Indeed, as the occupation prompted creative responses and a deeper seeing from Mansour and other artists of the region, they all arose like guiding stars, pointing the way.[20]

Whether in Banksy's graffiti on a petrol station or at a random intersection, or in Mansour's work in cultural memory and symbols of hope displayed at the Walled Off Hotel art gallery, I saw that the art tells the story of the current Herod and his collaborators and enforcers. Here, the advent storytellers are honest about Herod, and also honest about the presence of stars that we follow to find hope in hard places.

◆ ◆ ◆

Artwork like Mansour's speaks to political reckoning. It is the kind of reckoning we also witness in the Matthew narrative, as the magi offer gold, frankincense, and myrrh to the Holy Family.[21] As they entered the home, the magi greeted the mother and child, then prostrated themselves in a gesture of humility and honor by which they acknowledged the *true* King of the Jews. To reduce this act to only a religious ritual or a spiritual moment misses the point—the point that made Herod shudder. The magi dared to worship a rival ruler; they dared to acknowledge him as the true heir to the title "king."

When the magi left the house, they found a place to stay the night. A dream warned them of Herod's intentions, which they had likely suspected already. They would not play into Herod's hands nor put the young king in peril.

Taking leave of Bethlehem of Judea, the magi followed an alternate route home, a clandestine exit—their journey made, this time, without the assistance of a star.

In the telling of Advent, it's easy to miss the political intrigue in the magi's visit to the child. Often the story is told as a worship narrative, in which foreign sages travel from the East to worship Jesus, validating his place as the true Prince of Peace. But truer to this story is a star, a birth, a narrative that sends the magi home with visions of liberation for their land too.

❖ ❖ ❖

The first advent delivered a sign of tangible hope for people near and far: Judeans, Galileans, Persians. Maybe in Bethlehem, today a city of church bells alongside calls to prayer, this hope is more tangible among Christians and Muslims living as neighbors—embodying the lingering hope on offer for all, still.

In today's wearied world, hungry from east to west with the hunger of magi and shepherds alike for relief to come from a different kind of king, another sort of peace is familiar to us. It's a hunger that artists like Sliman Mansour portray as they, like stars, energize our resistance and offer direction to our deepest hopes.

The star of the first advent connects to ordinary people and a hard political and economic landscape. It is, for outsiders, a guide to a newborn king, a reminder that if hope can be birthed in Judea, it can be birthed in Persia too.

9

EVEN AFTER GOD ARRIVED

*The Holy Family, Mother Rachel,
and the Slaughter of the Innocents*

Bethlehem and Egypt | Matthew 2:13–18

Even after God arrived in the form of a baby, tense political dynamics continued. Economic hardship continued.
The entire region remained under threat. The new king
was born. Angels sang, shepherds visited, a star led magi
from the East to worship this child. Yet in the thick of
night, the Holy Family was forced to flee, seeking refuge
across a border in a foreign land.

Even after God arrived, there remained reason to
lament, as another massacre occurred, another traumatic
event visited upon the landscape and upon the families
who called Judea home.

Advent calls us to wrestle honestly with this truth:
troubles don't disappear just because Jesus arrived. The
world is still harsh and riddled with injustice. And Matthew knew it. He wrote his Gospel after the destruction
of the temple and the sacking of Jerusalem by the Roman

colonizers in 70 CE. Despite the birth, death, and resurrection of Jesus, things seemed like more of the same: empires and their economies exerting oppressive tactics with persistent and reactive force.

Lament remains the appropriate response to a world not immediately changed by God's arrival, and grief the honest response to the human experience even after God embodied our flesh and frame. Matthew tells of atrocities even in the wake of incarnation.

Even after the arrival of Jesus, when God's incarnation and theodicy are joined in the first advent and in all those since, we who seek to embody God's peace on earth respond to the perpetual invitation into places of pain.

After the birth of the heralded Prince of Peace, the advent story unfolds with refugees, infanticide, and collateral damage for those in the villages of Judea.

❖ ❖ ❖

After the magi depart, an angel appears once again to Joseph in a dream. The midnight messenger instructs him to hurry and take the mother and child to Egypt.[1] Herod is on the cusp of a rampage aimed at the child. Immediately Joseph obeys, fleeing with his family that very night. No time taken for long goodbyes with family or neighbors; no time to plan their route or to pack much, save some clothes and food left over from the previous day. Maybe they traveled with unleavened bread like their ancestors once did.[2]

The magi departed quietly to Persia, taking a less-traveled road. The Holy Family departed in the dark of night for Egypt, where they sought sanctuary.

For most families in the region, the morning dawn was a time to make daily bread for their loved ones. And for most on this particular morning, there was no warning. But Joseph took Mary and their child away from Bethlehem, and they became yet another refugee family fleeing a brutal regime. Jesus the refugee relied on the hospitality of Egyptians to stay safe when home was no longer secure.

It is a matter of human calculation as to when home becomes "the mouth of a shark," as Warsan Shire writes in one of her many poems about home, immigration, and seeking refuge in a dangerous world.[3] The daily duress of life under the empire could be enough to force one family to consider migration. The economic stresses or eventual land loss might push others to leave their home. Or, like Joseph, the threat of imminent peril triggers an immediate flight elsewhere, almost anywhere, to secure safety for one's family. The God who became a refugee holds deep compassion for those forced to make similar choices; it is in God's personal story, the memory embedded in God's own body.

❖   ❖   ❖

Herod knew that no matter what he tried, he would never be a beloved leader of the Judean people. No elaborate refurbishing of the temple could win their affections. And nothing would convince them that his roots and commitments were actually Jewish. His insecurities mounted. He knew that a messianic hope was growing among the Jews, and that disdain for his kingship was increasing their hunger for another king—perhaps this one, somewhere in the hills of Judea.

The birth of Jesus made Herod a threat to all the inhabitants of Roman Palestine. His paranoia provoked, Herod would likely do anything to quash the rumor or the young rival—putting everyone in harm's way. The magi tricked Herod. When they failed to return to the palace to give him news of the new king, their deception prompted him to ferret out the details on his own. Desperate to put an end to this rival king, and willing to be no wise man's fool, he ordered the murder of all male children under the age of two in Bethlehem and the surrounding region.

Herod's militias soon swept through the entire area in pursuit of the young rival. But far from a mission of precision, it left Bethlehem awash in blood, the epicenter of infanticide, and even surrounding towns were not spared.

When Herod's men hunted for boys of a certain age to slay, pressing family members and neighbors to give up the whereabouts of Judea's youngest sons, more blood ran in the streets as men and women who refused to comply were also killed. The death count included those

righteous ones who tried to hide and defend the innocents. Among them would have been Zechariah.

When the militia came to Ein Kerem, the village of
the righteous priest, he and his wife hid their son because
he was under two years old. Tradition remembers Elizabeth hiding in a subterranean space with infant John.
Zechariah, likely at the door, refused to let the soldiers in,
or blocked the road trying to divert them from his son's
hiding place. John remained hidden and survived the
massacre, but legend insists that Zechariah was targeted
and died in Herod's war against the sons of Bethlehem
and Judea.

As I read the Matthean narrative, I was struck to
notice for the first time that we don't hear of Jesus ever
returning to Bethlehem. He travels to nearby Jerusalem,
but not to the ancestral home of his father. In a sense,
this feels like the one place he didn't visit, which suggests
intention. I continued to wonder if it was due to the guilt
of the massacre in his name that he carried into his adult
life.

After passing through Bethany, where Mary, Mar-
tha, and Lazarus lived, maybe he hesitated when he came
to the edge of Bethlehem. Did he remember the stories
his mother told him of the time they left under cover of
darkness when others, like Zechariah, were left to fend
for themselves and try to protect their children? Jesus's
body, like all human bodies, must have held the trauma.
Part of incarnation was the loss of lives in his name.

I imagine that Jesus lived with his own sense of sadness that he was the child Herod sought, the reason for the post-advent slaughter. He got out with his life, and his father survived. But many others did not. And maybe every time he traveled south, the knowledge needled him—and he walked around Bethlehem to avoid his own lingering advent ache.

◆ ◆ ◆

Advent is the subversion of imperial power. As such, advent will always confront earthly empires, bringing God's disarmed peace, which arrives like a baby to an ordinary couple in an insignificant town on the edge of the empire. And the cycle of advent and atrocities in its aftermath continues as we opt for familiar modes of human power: the Pax Persica, the Pax Romana, and now the Pax Americana have all purported to be substitutes for God's peace. Only when advent is the final word will empires and their economies cease and the meek at last inherit the land.[4] Only when we find ourselves summoned by God alongside ordinary priests, barren or abused women, shepherds, tradesmen, and foreigners participating in God's subversive peace campaign, can we incarnate another kind of peace, can we inherit the land.

Prophets like Isaiah told of this subversive peace through poetry, igniting the imagination of Israel. But in the advent narratives where God takes on our very flesh to inhabit the human story, we see what defying the powers of this world could look like. In the incarnation, we see the possibility of embodying peace.

If violence begets more violence, as history reveals with little ambiguity, then what is the antidote? And how will the arrival of a defenseless baby as the picture of divine kingship set our imagination on a new trajectory for peace? Can we incarnate a regime without a corresponding military? Can we incarnate a regime that doesn't extract tribute and taxes from the peasantry? More to the point of advent, how can we imagine ourselves as part of such a weapon-free campaign?

The advent narratives stretch our sensibilities, pulling us from the status quo we are accustomed to, toward an utterly different embodiment of peace and salvation. It may not even be the deliverance Jews most hoped for when they dreamed of a Davidic leader coming to vanquish the foreigners, punishing rivals as similar powers have done for generations.

While Jesus was born in Bethlehem, the tender green shoot of an ancient lineage—of Jesse's old, dry tree stump—he was not what most expected. A savior who arrived without an army, he invited people to participate in their own liberation by living by a different story. By living an advent ethic. God recruits us to be advent practitioners, intentionally disarming our violent tendencies and cultivating abundant capacity for the ebb and flow of lament and hope.

❖ ❖ ❖

Among those who live under occupation in Jerusalem are people like Nafez Assaily, whose story I discovered through a local friend and peacemaker. The culture of violence shaped his childhood, much as it did that of young Mary in Galilee. Meeting that incessant conflict with resistance proved formative for Nafez as he grew up in the Occupied Territories. From Jerusalem to Nablus and eventually to Hebron, he witnessed the spear tip of hostility directed at his community. It would be understandable if he had succumbed to the weight of hardship, broken and bitter. But as Mary sang out her song of resistance in the hills of Judea, so Nafez held a different ethic and expectation for his land—a nonviolent one.

While attending university in Nablus, Nafez encountered for the first time the philosophy of nonviolence practiced by Gandhi. As he watched a movie about Gandhi's life and nonviolent action in India for one of his classes, Nafez wondered if Gandhi's method could be an answer to the Palestinian situation. His personal exploration turned into a commitment to live as an advocate for nonviolence in his homeland—an inclination that hinted of the mothers of advent, Mary and Elizabeth, who also imagined a future peace free of violence.

Over the next set of years, my friend and I would often return to Nafez's story. I learned that he had begun local initiatives in Hebron and the surrounding villages to teach nonviolence. He believed that training Palestinians in nonviolence had to be very practical and that he needed to offer tools that would help them resolve the basic struggles of their daily lives in nonviolent ways. This meant teaching families to understand and navigate their own city nonviolently, including its infrastructure and municipal leadership. His commitment to things concrete and practical resonated with me and the community development work my husband and I do. His wisdom felt both fresh and familiar.

When Nafez worked with kids, he showed them how to purchase good food (rather than the expired products flooding the markets from Israel) and how to avoid arguments with their parents at home.[5] He asked people about their life challenges and helped them create solutions that diminished frustration and agitation, always providing ways to steer clear of violence.

Nafez found that people learned best in the context of their own life, learning first how to manage family and work life without resorting to violence. As they do so, they slowly begin to embody a nonviolent approach to living in Palestine.

This approach requires patience, but he believes it is necessary as Palestinians absorb new information. Slowly and with small moves, people begin to see the benefits of nonviolent resolutions. Patience in the work is something Nafez considers a primary virtue. Creating a culture of nonviolence takes time—maybe even generations.

He, like other friends in the region, shares a hope for a Gandhi-like figure to emerge from among these children, one who can be a positive catalyst.[6]

In this work with children, one of Assaily's best tools is books. In 1996 he began the Library on Wheels for Non-violence and Peace.[7] Some villages are so remote that he could only get there by donkey with a saddlebag full of books. As he traveled, he loaned kids books featuring stories of nonviolence. Returning weeks later, he exchanged them for new books, and in this way he cultivates children's exposure to new ideas, widening their perspective of possible responses to frustration within their family or community. As someone whose life has been changed by books, by meeting stories of justice and peacemaking in words on pages, I was profoundly moved when I heard about Nafez's work with children who had to travel through checkpoints. I could imagine boys, picture book in hand, reading stories of nonviolence distracting them from the soldiers. Or girls, engrossed in chapter books about Malala Yousafzai or another brave girl. This initiative instantly convinced me of his genius.

Nafez got to know the kids and their parents, and they often talked about real challenges in their community as he counseled them in nonviolent approaches to resolving matters. The children who first benefited from the program are now in their twenties. Some are leading nonviolent actions in their own communities, thanks to Nafez and his vision for peace.

In 2007 he created a program that distributed books to
Palestinian commuters.[8] The second Intifada had ended,
but the long wait at various Israeli checkpoints hadn't.
So Nafez partnered with bus drivers to provide reading
material for commuters enduring delays beyond their
control. He curated a collection of books of short stories
and lessons appropriate for the ride times, all of which
taught nonviolence. Some of the books were profiles of
the ancestors Joseph, Moses, and Jesus—models he saw
as responding to hard circumstances without resorting to
violence. Reading would, he hoped, be a good way to take
the edge off the wait, diffuse the frustration, and harness
that time into productive activity. It also struck a subversive note, showing the Israeli soldiers at the checkpoints
that Palestinians were making good use of their time, not
seething at the delays or looking for a fight.[9]

For more than three decades, Nafez Assaily has practiced the slow, steady work of nonviolence in hard, even
remote terrain. He embodies the patience of a true peacemaker. He exemplifies deep participation in God's peace
campaign, accepting advent's invitation. He is creating
a culture change toward peace, working in generational
arcs toward a future where justice can flourish.

❖ ❖ ❖

After Matthew tells of the slaughter of the innocents, several times he repeats the words *mother* and *child*.[10] As he
mentions the weeping of Mother Rachel for her children,

the vulnerability of many generations of mothers, sons, and daughters haunts this text.

As I read the text again, I imagine that this is another thing Mary pondered in her heart on the trek to Egypt, once the news of what happened in the wake of their departure reached her. Maybe she wept like Rachel for another generation of children lost to yet another empire. Maybe she wept like mothers weep still for the children of Gaza, Ramallah, and Bethlehem. Because it seems empires continue to come for our children, even as we live under new iterations of Caesar's so-called peace.

And while the mothers of Bethlehem and the nearby towns like Ein Kerem are not directly named by Matthew, they are certainly in view as the Gospel writer invokes the memory of Rachel, quintessential mother of Israel.[11] According to the prophet Jeremiah, she was inconsolable, much like the daughter of Zion (Jerusalem) in Lamentations, who found none to comfort her in her grief.[12]

Whether the loss of Jerusalem in 587 BCE or of those taken captive to Babylon or all the other atrocities that subsequently rocked the land, the grief was unrelenting. Rachel wept without ceasing. The slaughter of children in the aftermath of the first advent was now added weight to her grief. Maybe that's what Matthew hoped his readers would see—this fresh grief connected to the others preceding it.

But there is something else about Matthew's choice of text. Rather than point to the "Daughter of Zion" of

Lamentations to convey grief over more loss at imperial hands, he chooses the poem from Jeremiah. In doing so, he makes a subversive move to point toward hope. Rachel's bitter weeping for her children and refusal to be consoled are part of what is called "The Little Book of Consolation," a small missive of hope within Jeremiah's words and writings. In Matthew's use of these lines of the poem in perfect resonance with the bloodbath in Bethlehem, his readers are prompted to also recall God's response to Mother Rachel and an unexpected reversal— the promise that her children will return to her from captivity in foreign lands: "There is hope for your future, says the Lord: your children shall come back to their own country."[13] They will live, and thus she can celebrate the newness that God brings after seasons of devastation. What Matthew alludes to is a poem as heavy with promise as it is with pain.[14]

And in Rachel, Matthew chose the preeminent Mother of Suffering. Rachel waited years to marry Jacob after her father foiled their union. And then she struggled with barrenness. After she did give birth to a son, she saw him disappear at the hand of his brothers. In childbirth with her second son, she died. In her short life she carried lamentations that haunted the landscape for generations to come.

The memorial at Ramah, where Rachel was buried, stands as a reminder not only of her loss but of all other children lost too soon. In a subsequent season, Ramah would be the staging area for those children taken into Babylonian captivity.[15] It became a locus for losses remembered by Israel, a kind of memorial touchstone. With Rachel's bones in the soil of this place, it was a convergence of mother and land holding both lament for loved ones lost and grief for future generations.[16]

But Mother Rachel's loss was to be reversed generations beyond her own lifespan. Jeremiah writes that she, alongside other bereft mothers of the land, would rejoice in this family reunion initiated by God.[17]

This is the promised reversal that unravels empires, past and future. Jeremiah wrote about it as a plucking and then a planting, as the tearing down and then the building back. Later Isaiah would continue these themes, using words of exile and then return.

Then Matthew, drawing from the Jewish canon, reminds those who weep in Bethlehem that the next stanza in the reversals is the experience of God's slow but sure hope.

Tearing down, then planting; exile, then return; weeping, then meeting God's future—these reversals will arrive on another generation's horizon, and they are the reward for those faithful who lamented like Mother Rachel.[18]

❖ ❖ ❖

Advent's exhortation is to God's peace, birthed among ordinary people in hard landscapes. The message is as relevant now as it was in ancient Palestine. Embodying God's peace and living as a peacemaker amid troubled times—this is what the newborn king did. He incarnated another kind of peace for a world hemorrhaging with injustice.

This was no easy peace—it came with confrontations, abandonment by his followers, crucifixion. But that way of seeing the world and of living into it differently brought change, if slowly.

As long as there are empires based on human power, there will be the need for advent. Beyond holy days or holidays, advent is about the kind of power we choose to live out and embody on earth.

As long as there are land removals and home demolitions; as long as peace talks start, stop, and stall without advancing justice; as long as American-made bombs drop on Gaza from Israeli planes, we are called to cry out for advent. First Intifada, Second Intifada, and every other act of resistance until we embody advent's peace.

❖   ❖   ❖

Nafez Assaily says that creating a nonviolent culture begins at home, begins in your own village—before it ever looks like direct action. First, it is a disarming of violent tendencies in ourselves and in our own reactions to people and situations we encounter daily. When the work has been done within, then we have the tools to create changes that make for true peace.[19]

This call to disarm violence is a necessary ingredient of God's restorative justice and congruent with the imperatives of the first advent. We welcome this newborn God-with-us into our arms instead of reaching for weapons, instead of coming to blows with enemies. We tend the fragile newborn One given to humanity by God, as the hope for a new kind of kingdom, a different peace, and a future and lasting justice.

10

HOMELAND, BUT NOT A HOME

Holy Family, Return from Egypt

Nazareth | Matthew 2:19–23

The advent narratives remind us of the hard truth that empires keep coming. Even as one wanes, another emerges with the same violent tactics. The exodus from Egypt, while emancipating the Hebrews, did not end empire. The release of the captives from Babylon brought their return and the rebuilding of Jerusalem, but it did not end empire. One imperial force replaced another. God's arrival was the divine's most direct action yet. And still Rome remained a superpower for the decades that followed. Nor was it the final empire.

It isn't only that atrocities happened in the aftermath of the first advent, but that empires and their economies remained. A resignation regarding peace came with the question, Is Caesar's peace the only possible peace? And the status quo was set. If it was not one empire, it was another. If it wasn't one emperor, it was another. Advent tells us something else: Until the newborn king, in all his vulnerability and gentleness, is embraced, God's peace will be kept at bay. The promise of true peace is one no empire can keep.

We see this arc as Matthew offers the final details of his advent narrative. Joseph and Mary return to the land of Israel with their child. But their return to Bethlehem was complicated by another harsh ruler. Joseph's repatriation would be a retreat of sorts. He went instead to make a new home in Nazareth. Even there, no promise of safety held his family, given the tense nature of the Galilee region. Yet, they made their way north as newly-minted peacemakers in God's kingdom.

❖ ❖ ❖

As Herod had sensed his death approaching, he worried that no one would mourn him. So he rounded up regional leaders, those who would be missed and therefore mourned, and instructed his militia to kill those leaders upon his death. This assured him that the country would weep on the occasion of his death, one way or another. However, the plan was thwarted, and he alone died.

The occasion of Herod's death prompted a wave of rebellions across the region, especially in Galilee. Whiffs of hope stirred among the people, and they took the news of his death as an opportunity to push against the imperial yoke. With punishing force, Rome came in from the north, pounding the villages and towns of Galilee, notably Sepphoris, near Nazareth. So much loss in the wake of Herod's death called for lament, but it was no longer about him. It never was, really. It was the successive nature of imperial violence on full and painful display—daily oppression, the slaughter of the innocents in Judea, and eventually the violent revolt of the people and the inevitable imperial backlash.

Then, Matthew writes, Joseph had a third dream. For who knows how long he'd been a refugee in Egypt along with his family. Now the divine instruction came to take Mary and their son back to the land of Israel because Herod was dead.

Joseph took his family back toward home. But though Herod was dead, his son now ruled Bethlehem and was already garnering a reputation for ruthlessness akin to that of his father. Word traveled fast when Archelaus ordered troops into Jerusalem, who then killed three thousand inhabitants[1] to quell a riot as mourners protested an earlier murder, by Herod, of two religious teachers in the temple.[2] There was no reason to believe Archelaus would be a gentler ruler than his father.

Joseph understood that if word of his return to Bethlehem got out, Herod's son would likely seek revenge. Maybe their return would trigger another slaughter. The risk was too high. As if his own calculations were not enough, in yet a fourth dream the fears were confirmed. Once more, Joseph protected his family. And it would cost him. Forced to abandon his home in Bethlehem, and to avoid Judea altogether, he found his way to Galilee. He returned to his homeland, but not to his home.

❖ ❖ ❖

The last time I visited Bethlehem, we drove with Naïef past the Aida Refugee Camp. The camp clings to the edge of the town, wedged between Rachel's Tomb and the separation wall. Walking through the streets, you notice refugees from another atrocity, another forced flight from what was once home. No wonder they named the camp Aida, which means "she who will return"—indication of a fervent hope.[3] The residents of Aida left their villages during the Nakba, "catastrophe," in 1948, pushed out when Jewish immigrants from Europe arrived by the boatload after the Holocaust. As that tragedy's survivors looked for shelter and the new state of Israel was formed, Palestinian villagers were evicted—most by force.[4] Many fled with housekeys in hand and little else. Those keys became emblematic of the devastation that had beset Palestinian families. At the entry into Aida is the Key of Return, a massive black arch with a skeleton key sculpted at its top as a reminder for all who enter.[5]

Walking through the Key of Return arch and along the gray barrier walls, you can see resistance art that tells the story of martyrs and imprisoned fathers, rockets rained down on neighboring Gaza. Bullet holes in the wall authenticate the story of struggle. Messages encouraging steadfastness and hope for return also appear on various streets. The alleys are so narrow that the trucks with skunk water can barely fit through for the frequent dowsing of homes and community spaces shared by those who still dare to await return.

One intersection in Aida displays the names of all the villages where the inhabitants of Aida come from—and hope to return one day. The villages may be gone now, and the homes their keys once matched likely destroyed or occupied by Jewish families, but the village names live on in the art and in the memory of the displaced. Their keys, once functional, are now aspirational. The people cling to keys as heirlooms, where justice has not afforded them the opportunity to cling to inherited homes, land, and orchards. Still, they wait for what they now know is a slow justice.

❖ ❖ ❖

As the Holy Family made their way north for a new start in the small town of Nazareth, maybe it felt like they were living as ever-displaced people, unable to go to their preferred home. Maybe Mary remembered her little garden in Bethlehem, the corner of the yard where she could sit in the sun and sip her morning tea before another set of daily chores. Maybe she sometimes thought of her favorite stall in the market full of the sweetest figs and apricots. Maybe she smiled at the memory of the elderly woman who always added a few extra herbs to the basket with advice on how to use them to prevent one sickness or another—what a blessing she was during the final months of Mary's pregnancy. Along with the birth of her son and the magi's visit, Mother Mary likely pondered these things too.

But Nazareth was a place for those displaced from Jesse's tribe. Most had come by way of Babylon, after the captivity. Some made their way north from Judea looking for work, especially tradesmen hoping to secure a job on one of the many construction sites in Tiberias or Sepphoris, the latter closest to the town of the Nazarenes.[6] Joseph, Mary, and their son would be welcomed as kin since they were fellow branches of Jesse's tree, now transplanted into northern soil.

❖ ❖ ❖

They arrived to a turbulent time in Galilee, a tinderbox lit by the death of Herod. Revolts were unleashed across the region in the wake of the news. Finally free from Herod, hope for an overturn of power arose among the populace. Swift action could create the conditions for liberation from oppression, heavy taxation, and imperial meddling in their village life. Born was a season for messianic movements, bandits, and resistance fighters.[7]

Joseph and his small family circumvented the danger of Bethlehem and Archelaus, but moved right into the unrest and uprisings that were part of the whole region of Galilee. It is likely that Joseph, as a tradesman, found work with neighbors on a construction site in Sepphoris, a reasonable walk across the shallow valley from Nazareth. This put him at the center of Galilee, as Sepphoris was the administrative hub for the region, filled with government functionaries and tax collectors.

About this time, local revolutionaries brought the full weight of their resistance efforts to bear on Sepphoris, breaking into the building that held a weapons cache, attacking military forces stationed there, and disturbing the regular operations of the regime. The resisters sought to unseat the current power structure and reclaim their sovereignty. When Rome heard of the attempted insurrection, Caesar dispatched a legion from the north to punish Galilee and deal a final blow to resistance to Rome once and for all, delivering a lasting message to any who might again consider revolution.

When Rome's forces came to Sepphoris, they devasted the landscape. The people who could do so fled from the arriving legions. Those who remained became victims. The historian Josephus recounts the mass crucifixions of men, enslavement of children, and rape of women during this siege. The military also razed villages and destroyed fields, leaving only smoldering ash and the sound of wailing. No one was untouched. Those who didn't lose their lives lost sons and daughters, husbands and homes, land and neighbors. They witnessed the unforgettable, exactly as Rome had planned.

While Luke records one additional event in the life of Joseph, Matthew's narrative for him comes to a close.[8]

Perhaps Joseph was among those lost to the Roman advance on Sepphoris and surrounding villages.[9] Mary and her young son might have hidden with neighbors in a nearby cave. But maybe the day the Romans came, Joseph was trapped in Sepphoris, unable to get to them. Once silence fell upon Sepphoris, families waited for their loved ones to find their way home. Many never returned. This scenario may explain why Joseph does not appear in the Gospel stories beyond the advent narratives.

So for at least part of his childhood, Jesus grew up without Joseph, in a landscape littered with reminders of men lost, his own father likely among them. Even he didn't escape the heartbreak or the haunting presence of empire. He was not spared the personal trauma of loss or the difficult learning of how to live without a loved one. Jesus not only inhabited a traumatized landscape; he was a victim of imperial trauma from a young age. Before he carried the cross through the narrow streets of Jerusalem, his body carried loss in Nazareth.

This is incarnation. Not inhabiting a body of privilege exempt from poverty and violence, but living in a body thick with the trauma common to most in Galilee and Judea.

God incarnated this pain in his own human body. It became a part of his human experience and is now woven into God's eternal memory. Jesus had a lifelong relationship with Roman soldiers and those who colluded with the empire that killed so many of his neighbors and relatives and perhaps even his own father. Consider the deeper power, then, of Jesus's words of love, forgiveness, and mercy in light of his own trauma. To love those who wrought suffering on his family and himself is divine love. His human grief pierced straight into the heart of God, and God's love came in response.

❖ ❖ ❖

Hammers abound—those who reach for violence, like the Maccabees once did. In the West Bank, the signature of the Maccabean hammer is ubiquitous in the form of cement barriers and checkpoints, Israeli soldiers with machine guns slung across their chests, and coils of razor wire throughout the region. To the hammers, every Palestinian appears to be a nail.

But there are branches too: those who hope for justice and try to live at peace with their neighbors amid the daily obstacles of the occupation. Perhaps they are less obvious, tender leaves gently rustling in the breeze, barely noticeable. But rooted there, like the terraced hills lined with olive trees, the branches wave for reprieve from another punishing regime.

When I last visited Palestine, I made my way to one such place on an October morning. My friend Naïef took another friend and me to a small village called Kafr Malik, deep in the West Bank. We pulled up to a small plot of land, and Tahany came from among the olive trees to greet us. Because we arrived while the olives were ripe, we were welcomed to help in the harvest.

We joined about twenty family members already at work. Khalid and his brothers balanced on ladders, using hand rakes to shake olives loose from the top branches of the massive trees. The purpled fruit rained down like Ping-Pong balls through the many boughs, landing on tarps where Tahany's sisters sat. Instructions for picking and sorting the olives came right along with introductions to the family. As Tahany translated, explaining how we met as neighbors in the United States and our kids attended school together and played together at the park most weekends, the women listened and nodded even as their hands never stopped working.

Khalid came down from his perch atop the ladder to make a fire and boil some sage tea. He remembered it was something I had enjoyed in their stateside home. I had vowed to not drink it again until we were together in Palestine, so when he handed us cups of the aromatic tea, I began to cry. Sipping the sage tea with Tahany under the ancient olive trees felt like communion, our friendship taking on a deeper hue as we drank together in her homeland after the obstacles had made our reunion a challenge in previous years.

For hours we picked, sorted, sifted, and talked endlessly. Stories told in Arabic were aided by some English translation, but the laughter was a universal language. Her sons, whom I hadn't seen in nearly seven years, joined us under the trees, and I marveled at their growth. I met her sweet daughter, a toddler, for the first time and watched her rest in her mother's arms whenever Tahany dared to stop sorting olives or supervising us. Lunch was served under the canopy of trees—makluba, stuffed grape leaves, Arabic salad, and incessant conversation.

When Tahany translated, we heard variations of the same narrative from each person. They love their land. They desire the best for their families and neighbors. "We are peaceful," they said as if in unison. But the days are hard, with complications caused by the occupation: the injustices slow down everything from grocery shopping to commuting to town. And almost every request to go to Jerusalem to pray during Ramadan or to Jaffa to visit the sea is denied. Tahany told me that Khalid's mother, who sat in a chair among us, still holds a key to her home in a northern village she can no longer even visit. I sensed her resignation about ever being able to return, but a hope abides for relief from daily troubles in Kafr Malik, even as things remain hard for everyone under Israel's control.

The day ended with all of us under one tree, huge and ancient. The family said it was at least a thousand years old. The men took to the ladders; the women laid out the tarps one last time and began collecting the olives. Incessant laughter energized bodies otherwise tired and sore from hours of labor. A euphoria embraced the lot of us as we gathered one last time, a joyful crescendo as we finished a day of harvesting, as generations before have done. I felt the hospitality of being invited into a tradition stewarded by generations of families, of being embedded for a day in an ancient rhythm.

Occupation makes life harder, but harvest days like this one persist. Empires rise and fall over and over again, but this olive tree stands a thousand years later as a testament to a rugged steadfastness and the capacity of its roots to grip the soil despite imperial hardship. It is equally true for the families tending the orchards, planting and harvesting for generations. Empires come and colonize, announcing their own version of peace, but the meek endure. The word of Jesus in Matthew's Gospel seemed to echo in the olive grove: that the meek will inherit the land.[10] Watching Tahany's family work together on that final tree as the sun set behind the hills and the air chilled, I experienced a swell of joy that felt old and somehow golden. I bore witness to the beauty of the meek that day in Kafr Malik.

Once we made our way to Tahany's house, she made us strong dark Arabic coffee. "It is so hard to live here," she said. "There are checkpoints that can be closed without notice for any reason—or no reason at all. Sometimes I am in the car with my children and groceries, and we are stuck at a checkpoint for hours. The food spoils before we even get home." Only a few cars in their entire village have permits to drive on the road to Ramallah, because it is so expensive to get the Israeli-approved plates. Our conversation that evening continued, with more talk of hardship, yet they also shared their hunger to live at peace with others, even Israelis.

As I listened, I was struck by the alternating words—*hardship* and *peace*. Over the years, I have heard the meek of Palestine speak these words often, not only to each other but to anyone willing to listen. They are quick to point out that not all residents of the West Bank are involved in direct action. Many are the meek, those who remain from generation to generation. And their very survival and steadfast commitment to the land are a confounding peace to the empires of today.

❖ ❖ ❖

Jesus heralded the meek ones as true inheritors of the land. Teaching on a hillside in Galilee when he was now a mature adult, he reached to Psalm 37, making an ancient hope contemporary. The psalmist offers the first biblical text to say that the meek will inherit the land despite all evidence to the contrary. The opening image in the psalm instructs the worshippers to not be vexed by evil ones because they will wither like the grass, they will one day fade away.[11] Instead, the text directs the worshipper: trust in God and continue to do good. This practice of good included abiding (a dedication to staying) in the land. "Take delight in the Lord, and [God] will grant you the desires of your heart," the psalmist famously says. In the context of roiling violence and economic turmoil, possibly the roughshod days of the Maccabees, what most peasants desired was the end of imperial warfare.[12] They wanted to live on their ancestral land untouched by violence and free from the heavy burden of indebtedness. Their heart's desire was peace.

When Babylon took the elite into captivity, they left behind those they deemed unimportant. Those who remained in the smoldering ruins of Jerusalem were the meek ones. They had nowhere else to go. But when the military left, the land was at last theirs. Perhaps this is what the psalmist had in mind, singing of the meek inheriting the land one day. Those with roots coiled into the soil of Palestine would one day lay claim to it again, despite the machinations of empire.

The same psalmist reminded the people that empires like Assyria, Babylon, and Persia had come and gone. The Syrian empire of Antiochus Epiphanes that the Maccabees struggled against also loomed large in the moment, but then faded like the grass. Perhaps when Jesus reached for Psalm 37 generations later, he wanted to assure those gathered in the agitated landscape of Galilee that day of their history, and of the deep hope they could hold on to amid the Roman occupation. In returning to Psalm 37, he reactivated an ancient hope; in essence, he told them to keep hope alive.

The meekness Jesus evoked wasn't about genteel people keeping Caesar's peace. The meek were the survivors of brutal empires and their economies. They were those with no resources to relocate, no option but to remain under dire conditions. So it was the meek who survived despite the trauma inflicted by the empire. The meek outlasted empires time and time again. As Jesus looked into the eyes of his fellow Galileans and invoked the psalm, he said that they (or their kin) would outlast Rome.

This long view of history informs a deeper understanding of what it meant when Jesus said the land would be inherited by the meek ones. According to Mitri Raheb, a Bethlehemite, writer, and Palestinian theologian, the meek are those left behind. They are the remnant after an empire departs, which they all eventually do.[13] Raheb said this realization transformed his relationship with the iconic sermon of Jesus: as a Palestinian living under occupation, he found that it offered him and the Palestinian people around him a word of needed hope.

Raheb speaks with honesty and hope about the region. Yet he knows better than most that life remained hard even after the arrival of Jesus to his hometown. Raheb illustrates the hardship in one of his books, where he wrote about his own father's struggle living under multiple governing powers without ever leaving Palestine.

Born in 1905, when Bethlehem was under the control of the Ottoman Empire, Raheb's father was issued citizenship papers. When he was a teenager, he became a citizen of the British Mandate and was issued a Palestinian passport. In 1948, when Bethlehem became part of Jordan, he became a citizen of the Hashemite Kingdom. He died in 1975 under occupation with an identity card issued by Israel.[14] In one lifetime he survived four empires.

The advent story names the reality imperial powers inflicted on families like Raheb's over decades—or centuries. The Gospels do not tell of an easy or quick peace, but of hard-borne hope as the meek endure hardship under one empire and then the next.

When Jesus pulls the thread of Psalm 37 into his Sermon on the Mount, he acknowledges the long history of empires in his homeland and sings the same song of hope that Mary sang as he looks out across the hillside and sees the meek ones. In doing so, he anticipates families like the Raheb clan, still surviving future empires. They will outlast Rome and any subsequent imperial force, Jesus declares; the land will at last be the inheritance of the meek.

This is the hope I carry as I write from the advent narratives, that the meek ones battered by perpetual cycles of violence, compounded by indebtedness and dispossession, will inherit the land. And those who inherit the land are the ones who live into the complexity and hope of advent peace.

❖ ❖ ❖

While in Bethlehem, Claude and I shared lunch with Sami Awad, a Palestinian Christian who has been working toward peace for more than twenty years from his base on Star Street.[15] We ate together, overlooking the crescents, crosses, and settlements that dotted the landscape. We asked him, an expert practitioner in the region, what he considered the way forward for peace in this hallowed land he calls home. He sat back in the wooden chair and then took a long, slow breath.

"I don't know," he sighed. "I stay out of politics—there are no answers to be found there. Neither side has a good plan," he relayed flatly.

"Then how do you work for peace?" Claude pushed, one practitioner to another. My husband's voice betrayed his own confusion at Sami's answer. Here was a seasoned peacemaker, seemingly holding a naïve position, when political strategies for change had been seen as the necessary way forward.

"I just keep connecting people," he responded.

Indeed, the core of Sami's work all these years has been creating spaces where people connect across fractured lines. He brings Israeli and Palestinian youth together, brings the devout of all three Abrahamic faiths together in common initiatives, and hosts visitors from foreign lands, introducing them to the local people of Bethlehem.

Still the answer felt unsatisfactory. Claude and I hungered for a better one. Sensing our disappointment, Sami turned the conversation toward our schedule for the coming days. "You should visit Hebron, Aida Refugee

Camp, go enjoy some falafel at Afteem's." He pulled out his phone and began dialing. "Good news! I have a friend who can drive you to Hebron tomorrow morning."

Claude and I have returned to that conversation on Star Street many times since. How do you find the energy to keep working for peace when the support dries up? How do you cling to hope when the occupation is as entrenched as the settlements ringed round the city? Our time with Sami was good, but left us with disturbing questions.

Now, years later and with advent explorations in view, I find myself circling back. Maybe Sami was right. Connecting people is a work of continued hope, each connection an act of resistance against the status quo of occupation, injustice, and futility. Each introduction, resisting isolation. Every gathering he hosts between Palestinians and Israelis, a seeding of the soil for a different future. Maybe every conversation creates the possibility of a new reality to come, new facts on the ground. He is weaving the fabric of God's peace—which is the practice of hope in hard times. He doesn't know what it will look like when the imperial cycle breaks, but he is preparing the ground for it just the same.

In this way, Sami follows the trajectory set by the first advent. Like Mary, Elizabeth, the shepherds, and the magi, he practices hope, knowing that God's peace will inaugurate a just world. He does not doubt the end of the empires because he knows the God who will defeat them all. So, with another deep breath, he makes another call, another connection, another step in hope.

❖ ❖ ❖

The advent narratives demand we take the political and economic world of Roman Palestine seriously. The Gospel writers named the empires of Caesar and Herod not for dramatic effect; they didn't mention a census or massacre for literary flourish. The Gospel writers used contextual markers to describe in concrete ways the turmoil of the times that hosted the first advent.

It is this very context that makes the advent narratives contemporary—whether in Israel-Palestine or lands beyond. Our troubled times, shaped by all manner of injustice, cause continued suffering, making the loud cries of lament and cries for peace timely, as they are answered by advent.

These narratives remind us that the birth of Jesus did not change the facts on the ground immediately. The first advent set in motion a new possible reality for the meek, like Zechariah and Elizabeth, Mary and Joseph, and a few shepherds. But societal transformation was not quick to come. That would require more time and collaboration with God's unfolding peace campaign, of which Luke and Matthew will have much more to say in the rest of their Gospel narratives about the life of Jesus.

After Jesus's birth, after the magi left covertly, the Holy Family fled for safety to Egypt. More innocent blood spilled in the streets of Bethlehem. Joseph, Mary, and their child returned as internally displaced people with a hometown too hostile to host them. And losses kept coming, the aftermath of the first advent littered with atrocities. Luke and Matthew knew it; so did their first-century audience. Now so do we.

An Advent faith is one that is buoyed by a generational hope, a long view of history combined with an equally long view of the future. It recalls that God spoke a word, and by divine fiat, there was light. But when God was clothed in human skin, navigating our terrestrial landscape, transformation took longer to enact. It is not impossible, as Gabriel said, just slower. So we join God with generational patience, knowing that making peace takes hard work and much time. But the advent narratives set our trajectory toward God's peace manifest on earth, both now and not yet.

These advent narratives reveal the Incarnation as more than God entering a human frame. They are also the revelation of God engaging with human trauma of a specific place and specific people. God experienced the excruciating reality of empires and economies from the position of the weak and powerless ones. God absorbed loss and pain in that body.

The Incarnation positions Jesus among the most vulnerable people, the bereft and threatened of society. The first advent shows God wrestling with the struggles common to many the world over. And from this disadvantaged stance, Jesus lives out God's peace agenda as a counter-testimony to Caesar's peace.

This is the story of advent: we join Jesus as incarnations of God's peace on this earth for however long it takes. God walks in deep solidarity with humanity, sharing in our sufferings and moments of hope. Amid our hardship, God is with us. Emmanuel remains the name on our lips in troubled times.

Advent isn't the acceptance of status-quo peace, but an incarnation of God's peace that we live in the world. The peacemakers formed by advent are those who resist empire, who practice hospitality with neighbors, and who enter into solidarity with God in the work of liberation for everyone.

May there be calm, bright nights ahead for the peacemakers, the meek, and all people God accompanies through advent still.

CONTINUATIONS

You have reached the end of this book, but not the end of the story. The advent narratives of Luke and Matthew form the early pages of their Gospels and set the context for Jesus's birth. But both Gospels have so much more to say about the hope-filled witness of Jesus on earth. They continue to tell the story of Jesus's life and his pursuit of justice, incarnating God's peace campaign in Galilee and beyond. In each Gospel we watch Jesus, energized by hope, confronting the empire.

That Jesus, born into a traumatized landscape and to a family that suffered under the weight of an occupation, presents a new kind of king wracked by the pain of empire: family members lost, stigma suffered, homes and homeland stolen. Embedded in the deepest memory of God is the sting of trauma. And this is what also infuses the Gospel narratives with hope. The God who experienced this particular pain knows how to redeem it.

This God-with-us will not forget our shared human experience. God will transform the world and all its brokenness, from incarnation to resurrection to a land the meek want to inherit, free of imperial violence. Only a God who knows and shares our pain can ultimately transform it.

It is this hope that energizes me as the Gospels continue their telling of the story that, in the end, empires don't stand a chance against this God. And it's a hope that energizes Palestinian Christians like Mitri Raheb, pastor and resident of Bethlehem. Raheb, familiar with life under occupation, reflects on what that hope means: "Holding to a hopeful vision in the context of war gives hope a new meaning. It is no longer something we see but rather something we practice, something we live, something we advocate, something we plant."[1]

Advent was never just about seeing the star over Bethlehem, but about practicing hope in hard landscapes, where hope isn't what we see—it's what we do. The advent narratives offer us a place to look as we begin our own practice of hope, as we trust God to break the cycle for good.

Each reversal in the advent narratives is a seed tossed into the soil, placed for hope to take root. Zechariah, Elizabeth, Mary, Joseph, and the shepherds are the grassroots practitioners showing us the hope that erodes empires. Among the tools we are given by the first advent in Palestine are hospitality, solidarity, and nonviolence—ready for the hopeful to use as we subvert the empires God will one day bring to an end.

As the magi don't just see the star from the East and marvel at it, we learn from them to act in hope and follow the star that guides us. We travel in the light of that star, in and through the trajectory of the advent story toward—always—resurrection!

ACKNOWLEDGMENTS

Writing a book during a pandemic presented tangible and intangible challenges to writing as usual. Being deprived of my regular writing space, a local café, for months on end interfered with the routine and ritual that shaped my previous work. That's tangible. But then there were the daily attempts to think clearly and creatively amid the chaos of the pandemic, the anxieties of the unknowns and confusion about the rules of engagement for this unprecedented season. The intangibles clouded my mind too often. That I completed this book is a testament to those who accompanied me from beginning to end, even as the pandemic remains our reality.

I can name the people who weathered this writing season with me, I can mostly describe the ways they buoyed me as I took pen to paper amid the storm. And then there are the intangible ways they held me that I can't quite articulate because those ways are still shrouded in the pandemic haze. I just know I was accompanied in ways that now seem both mysterious and miraculous. All I can say is a thank you that feels too thin to match the bread in the wilderness they offered me.

ACKNOWLEDGMENTS

But here is what I can say...

Thank you to Annie Rim, Elie Pritz, and Lil Copan. Your steadfast companionship protected me from the worst of my insecurities and the potential loneliness of this season. You each offered encouragement rooted in rigorous honesty, laced with patience and kindness. Your company felt like communion at times, the sacrament I needed along the advent road.

Thank you to the loyal laureates, the best writing group a person could ever hope to belong to. Jessica Goudeau, Stina Kielsmeier-Cook, D.L. Mayfield, Amy Peterson, Christiana Peterson, I'm honored you've walked with me through all three of my books.

Thank you to those who showed up often with their enthusiasm and genuine interest in me and the book: Kaitlin Curtice, Nicole Miller, Sherry Naron, Sean and Paige Whiting, and Idelette McVicker. I could always hear you cheering me on!

Thank you to Fadi Kattan, my connection to Bethlehem during the pandemic. I intended to stay at the Hosh and write part of this book from Star Street—but then the pandemic hit. So your reflections from the markets, the emptied streets, the quiet Manger Square kept me tethered to the place as I remained afar. Your recipes so generously shared allowed the aromas of Palestine to fill my kitchen, and always your kindness amid the hardship in your hometown. Thank you for the hospitality that crossed continents.

ACKNOWLEDGMENTS

Thank you to Sliman Mansour for allowing us to use your provocative image, The Flight to Egypt, for the cover of this book. Your powerful artwork is only outmatched by your generosity and kindness.

Thank you to my friends at the Starbucks at Grand & Reems. When the café was open, you kept me company—and caffeinated—as we worked from the early morning hours of each day. You are a stellar crew—keeping up our spirits amid a pandemic, nonetheless! Absolutely essential.

And at last, thank you to Claude Nikondeha, my beloved. You make this all possible in a plethora of ways I could never fully articulate. You are the best partner, and you embody so much of the advent goodness I attempted to capture in these pages.

Advent 2021
Bujumbura, Burundi

NOTES

Beginnings

1 Bargil Pixner, *With Jesus through Galilee according to the Fifth Gospel* (Rosh Pina, Israel: Corazin, 1992).

Chapter 1

1 1 Maccabees 1:20–24.

2 1 Maccabees 1:25–28. The lament was communal—"Israel mourned deeply in every community . . ."—and impacted everyone. The lament was also total, like a stop order on all celebrations and on any business-as-usual.

3 "None to comfort" is like a drumbeat through the first poem of Lamentations. Lamentations 1:2, 9, 17, 21.

4 Lamentations 3:22–23.

5 1 Maccabees 1:29–33.

6 1 Maccabees 2:7.

7 This might remind the reader of Abraham and Sarah, who likewise took matters into their own hands when it came to a promised heir. Sarah sent Hagar in to Abraham, since she herself was beyond childbearing years. They couldn't wait with hope any longer.

8 The Maccabean Revolt was not only a battle between the Seleucids and Maccabees. It was also a civil war of sorts between Jews open to Hellenization and those devoutly opposed to any such influence on communal life. There were many people in Israel, especially in the Galilee region, as we will see in a coming chapter, who did not side with the Maccabees. So both external and internal dynamics of Mattathias's revolt contributed to the darkness experienced by the Jews, no matter what province or what side of the battleline they inhabited.

9 This theology was popularized by G. E. Ladd and the Vineyard Church movement.

10 Memories of liberation are dangerous to empires, and when the Jewish people later fell under the power of a subsequent empire, Hanukkah was reframed in the Talmud as a celebration of a different miracle. So the story of the miraculous jar of oil that burned for eight days functioned as a subversive strategy allowing for continued celebration right under the nose of that

later occupying force. When our Jewish neighbors celebrate Hanukkah, they remind us of centuries of suffering under various empires, hard-fought victories, and moments of light that deserve to be seen and remembered. Later generations show us that subversion is a virtue also connected to the lighting of the eight candles on the menorah.

11 This series of protests against the Israeli occupation in the West Bank lasted from 1987 until the signing of the Oslo Accords in 1993.

12 Thomas L. Friedman, *From Beirut to Jerusalem* (New York: Farrar, Straus and Giroux, 1989).

13 The separation wall, known by many names, was Israel's response to a wave of suicide bombings perpetrated by Palestinians. Construction began in 2000 during the Second Intifada, or Palestinian uprising against the occupation. It is a massive concrete wall that reaches 26 feet at its highest point and stretches 125 miles between the lands of the two peoples, often veering into West Bank territory. It is controversial and has been deemed illegal according to international law by both the United Nations General Assembly and the International Court of Justice at The Hague.

Chapter 2

1 Luke 1:5 is a reference to Herod the Great, who ruled Judea from 37 to 4 BCE.

2 Octavian (soon to be known as Caesar Augustus) defeated Mark Antony and Cleopatra at the Battle of Actium in 31 BCE. This has traditionally marked the beginning of the *Pax Romana*.

3 Richard Horsley, *The Liberation of Christmas: The Infancy Narratives in Social Context* (Eugene, OR: Wipf & Stock, 2006), 68–69.

4 For more about poverty as a manifestation of violence, see L. Juliana Claassens, "Resisting the Violence of Precarity," in *Reclaiming Her Dignity: Female Resistance in the Old Testament* (Collegeville, MN: Liturgical, 2016), 102–105. This includes comment on how precarity impinges most heavily on women, for example barren women, especially germane to this chapter and to the consideration of Elizabeth.

5 Jubilee is an economic policy outlined in Deuteronomy 15, Leviticus 25, and the poetry of Isaiah 61, as well as on the lips of Jesus in Luke 4 as his inaugural sermon and description of his work.

6 Horsley, *The Liberation of Christmas*, 96–99.

7 At this time in history, children were expected and seen as a blessing. Barrenness prompted questions about the virtue of a family and created stigma around the woman.

8 Horsley, *The Liberation of Christmas*, 94–95.

9 Horsley, 96.

10 For more information on Razzouk Tattoo, go to www.razzouktattoo.com. See also Kelley Nikondeha, "The Pilgrim's Mark: A Coptic Tattoo Artist Marks the Journey to Jerusalem," *The Plough*, April 6, 2020, https://www.plough.com/en/topics/culture/art/the-pilgrims-mark.

11 Luke 1:8–10.

12 Robert Tannehill recommends seeing the prayers of Zechariah alongside those of Simeon and Anna, who offered collective prayers for "the consolation of Israel" and "redemption of Jerusalem," respectively (Luke 2:25, 38). *Luke*, Abingdon New Testament Commentaries (Nashville: Abingdon, 1996), 45.

13 Luke 1:14–15.

14 Luke 1:18.

15 According to Daniel 9 and 10, Gabriel appeared to Daniel in the temple and left him speechless as well. Faithful Jewish men would have known the story and seen the connection.

16 Isaiah 11:1.

17 God's "preferential option for the poor," a Catholic concept, dates back to the Jesuits in 1968 and is a term that was used by Pope Francis in his 2013 apostolic exhortation, *Evangelii Gaudium (The Joy of the Gospel)*, https://www.vatican.va/content/francesco/en/apost_exhortations/documents/papa-francesco_esortazione-ap_20131124_evangelii-gaudium.html. However, it is best articulated by Gustavo Gutiérrez in *A Theology of Liberation: History, Politics, and Salvation* (Maryknoll, NY: Orbis, 1971).

Chapter 3

1 There is not absolute agreement on Galilee as a restive region, but trusted scholars like Richard A. Horsley make a compelling case that I am inclined to accept as valid. See his work in *Jesus and the Politics of Roman Palestine* (Columbia: University of South Carolina Press, 2014); *Archeology, History, and Society in Galilee: The Social Context of Jesus and the Rabbis* (Harrisburg, PA: Trinity Press International, 1996); *Bandits, Prophets, and Messiahs: Popular Movements in the Time of Jesus* (Harrisburg, PA: Trinity Press International, 1985); and *The Liberation of Christmas*.

2 Galileans lived for eight centuries apart from Judea, with their own culture and history. King Solomon had given the ten cities

of Galilee away to fund his building projects. But the region was rejoined with Judea during the time of the Maccabees, though this was not an easy integration of the two different peoples. For more, see Horsley, *Archaeology, History, and Society*, 15, 19–27.

3   A similar dynamic can be seen in Isaiah 7:14–16. A woman's body is part of the determination of time: she will "conceive and give birth to a son." And the stopwatch continues with her child, who will grow to eat curds and honey and know right from wrong before the land is "deserted."

4   The root word of Nazareth and Nazorean is *netzer*, meaning "branch" in Hebrew. This refers to the stump of Jesse in Isaiah 11:1.

5   Betrothal was different from our modern concept of engagement. Betrothal was the first step in the marriage, the contract between families. To break a betrothal had legal and financial ramifications, unlike engagements of today. We will see Joseph wrestle with these ancient realities in chapter 7.

6   Pixner, *With Jesus through Galilee*, 16–19.

7   Mary's place of origin is uncertain. Some say her parents, Joachim and Anna, can be traced to Jerusalem. But another tradition has Mary growing up in Sepphoris, a prominent city in Galilee. And these aren't the only theories. However, Luke only mentions finding her in Nazareth.

8   Reza Aslan describes Nazareth as a village of about one hundred people, one well, and one bath. It doesn't appear in any ancient Jewish literature before the third century CE. It was "an inconsequential and utterly forgettable place." *Zealot: The Life and Times of Jesus of Nazareth* (New York: Random House, 2013), 25–26. Others, including Bargil Pixner and Richard A. Horsley, also note the town's smallness and relative insignificance.

9   John 1:46.

10 John 1:45.

11 I'm grateful to Elie Pritz for pointing this out to me as we walked through Nazareth and Sepphoris together. The iconic question was more likely about messianic expectation than the insignificance of Nazareth.

12 Luke 1:28.

13 Jane Schaberg mentions the figurative or symbolic use of "virgin" and of the divine conception employed by Matthew. Could Luke be doing likewise? *The Illegitimacy of Jesus: A Feminist Theological Interpretation of the Infancy Narratives* (San Francisco: Harper & Row, 1987), 66–67.

14 Something underreported in Gaza is the high levels of sexual abuse within families. Those who work in the region know

NOTES

that much of the trauma the men of Gaza have experienced is internalized and then taken out in the privacy of their homes in the form of rape and molestation, resulting in another layer of trauma: that of the abuse victims. The dynamic is as inescapable as Gaza itself. Everyone is trapped in cycles of trauma, bearing the marks of incessant abuse that can't be discussed within an honor/shame-based culture. It is not hard to imagine similar struggles in the turbulent Galilee of the first century, though no one would write it out.

15 The accusation of adultery was first written by Celsus at the end of the second century, though he did have an anti-Christian agenda. The allegation named a Roman solider, Panthera, as complicit in the affair. What I find interesting is that the allegation pulls from the regional memory of Syrian legionary soldiers who roamed Sepphoris, near Nazareth, around that time. Marcus J. Borg and John Dominic Crossan, *The First Christmas: What the Gospels Really Teach about Jesus's Birth* (New York: Harper One, 2007), 104.

16 Catholic biblical scholar Jane Schaberg, author of *The Illegitimacy of Jesus*, believed that the infancy texts of Luke and Matthew were about an illegitimate conception and not a miraculous virginal conception. She goes on to say that that the possibility of rape (as well as that of seduction or adultery) would be other ways to account for Mary's pregnancy. Schaberg, *The Illegitimacy of Jesus*, 1, 19. Her exploration of the texts in these directions was so controversial when published that someone set her car on fire in response.

17 Before living in Nabi Saleh, the Tamimi clan lived in Hebron for many generations. Yotam Berger, "'How Was Such a Fool Your U.S. Ambassador?' Tamimi Family Mocks Michael Oren's Secret Probe into Whether They're Real Palestinians," *Haaretz*, January 25, 2018, https://www.haaretz.com/middle-east-news/palestinians/.premium-ahed-tamimi-s-family-ridicules-israel-s-secret-probe-of-their-identity-1.5765380.

18 You can read about Nabi Saleh, the Tamimi family, and their protest movement in Ben Ehrenreich, *The Way to the Spring: Life and Death in Palestine* (New York: Penguin, 2016).

19 "'Skunk water' is an extremely foul-smelling liquid sprayed from water cannons. It induces nausea and takes days to wash off. It is sprayed over neighborhoods where protests happen, collectively punishing them," according to an exhibit description at The Walled Off Hotel Museum in Bethlehem.

20 As for damages to Nabi Saleh and its people, Bassem Tamimi said that in just the first fourteen months of protesting, 155

residents, including forty children, were injured; nearly every home had been damaged with gas grenades and other projectiles; seventy villagers, twenty-nine children, had been arrested; and six people were in hiding. Ehrenreich, *The Way to the Spring*, 15. Imagine this damage to a village of six hundred people, and this was only fourteen months into a multiyear series of nonviolent actions.

21 The first Intifada began in 1987 as a nonviolent movement against the Israeli occupation, but it grew into a more violent enterprise. The signature weapon was a stone, often hurled by a child, thus the moniker "children of the stones." *Intifada* means "shaking off," and the Palestinian people wanted to shake off their occupiers.

22 Ehrenreich, *The Way to the Spring*, 43.

23 Ahed Tamimi was released from prison on July 29, 2018. To read about Ahed and her connection to young Miriam of Exodus, see Kelley Nikondeha, *Defiant: What the Women of Exodus Teach Us about Freedom* (Grand Rapids: Eerdmans, 2020).

24 Lisa Loden, "Captive Sister" (unpublished), shared in personal correspondence with the author.

25 Borg and Crossan make note of the two mentions of "the Most High" in this passage: Luke was making a distinction with other gods, especially Roman deities, in which many people believed at the time. *The First Christmas*, 115.

26 Schaberg, *The Illegitimacy of Jesus*, 84.

27 Traumatized people either internalize or externalize their pain. The external manifestation is often sexual abuse within families and communities. This is what is happening across Gaza, as cycles of violence riddle communities with trauma and the resulting abuse that is taboo to talk about but is a real menace to women and children. This is according to Dr. Eyad El Sarraj, a Palestinian psychologist working in Gaza. See Elie Pritz, "Eyad El Sarraj, Israel/Palestine," *Peace Heroes* (curriculum), 2019; unpublished and used with author's permission.

28 Laurie King-Irani, "The Arab Capital of Israel," review of *Beyond the Basilica: Christians and Muslims in Nazareth*, by Chad F. Emmett, *Journal of Palestine Studies* 25, no. 3 (Spring 1996): 103–5, https://doi.org/10.2307/2538265.

Chapter 4

1 Luke 1:46–55.

2 Jane Schaberg notes that *meta spodés*, the Greek translation of the Hebrew "with haste," also hints at terror or trouble, carrying connotations of serious concern. Maybe an unexpected

pregnancy or turn of events had Mary upset, Schaberg speculates. *The Illegitimacy of Jesus*, 89.

3 While she was betrothed, as Luke has pointed out, the marriage would not be considered complete until she shared a home with her husband.

4 Luke 1:44.

5 Judges 5 and Judith 13.

6 Luke and his original audience would have known about Jael and Judith. Brittany E. Wilson, "Pugnacious Precursors and the Bearer of Peace: Jael, Judith, and Mary in Luke 1:42," *Catholic Biblical Quarterly*, 68, no. 3 (July 2006), 436–56.

7 Judges 4:21.

8 This ancient song was likely composed by Deborah not long after the original events. Tikva Frymer-Kensky on Deborah in *Women in Scripture*, ed. Carol Meyers (Grand Rapids: Eerdmans, 2000), 66–67.

9 The book of Judith is part of the Apocrypha and considered a fictitious book, in the vein of an extended parable.

10 Brittany E. Wilson says this is true of Mary, a logic I extend to include Elizabeth, who spoke the words of blessedness. *Pugnacious Precursors and the Bearer of Peace*, 438.

11 Richard Bauckham, *Gospel Women: Studies of the Named Women in the Gospels* (Grand Rapids: Eerdmans, 2002), 65.

12 Luke 1:44.

13 Genesis 18:12.

14 We will see this again on Easter Sunday, when the women are the first to encounter an empty tomb, and then to see a risen body. They became the first to wrestle with the reality of resurrection and find language for a risen Lord. They were the initial evangelists, first to their fellow disciples and then to the wider community. Luke's version of events makes it clear yet again that the women believed while the men, at first, did not. As with Zechariah, it took the men time to believe and join the resurrection conversations started by the women.

15 See Judges 5, 1 Samuel 2:1–10, Judith 16:1–17, and Exodus 15:21. For more about this tradition of women and song, refer to Bauckham, *Gospel Women*, 54. To consider Miriam's song of deliverance in particular, see Kelley Nikondeha, "Descendants of Miriam: Beating Out the Rhythms of Liberation" in *Defiant: What the Women of Exodus Teach Us about Freedom* by (Grand Rapids: Eerdmans, 2020).

16 Ein Kerem is the current village just outside of Jerusalem that tradition honors as the place of the visitation, the home of Zechariah and Elizabeth, the birthplace of John the Baptist.

NOTES

17 Luke 1:48–50.

18 Deuteronomy 22:23–27. This is the exegetical and analytical work of Jane Schaberg in *The Illegitimacy of Jesus*, 97–100. Her thesis is well researched and compelling.

19 Luke 1:52.

20 Mark 11:15–18; Matthew 21:12–13; John 2:14–15.

21 Mary Catherine Nolan, *Mary's Song: Living Her Timeless Prayer* (Notre Dame, IN: Ava Maria, 2001), 12.

22 Compare Isaiah 61:1–2 and Luke 4:16–19.

23 I am referring to the joint work and "jam sessions" of Parents Circle (https://www.theparentscircle.org/en/pcff-communities _eng/pcff-women_eng/jam-session_eng/), as well as to the Women's March (https://womensmarch.com/ and https://www. womensmarchfoundation.org/) and similar initiatives.

24 Mark 6:2–3.

25 Luke wants the readers to hear the echo of Genesis 21:6 and the neighbors celebrating with the once-barren woman.

26 Luke 1:63.

27 See the echo of Luke 1:66 in 2:19: "Mary treasured all these words [regarding her own son] and pondered them in her heart."

28 Robert C. Tannehill sees political freedom in Zechariah's words, especially in 1:71, 74. *Luke*, 41. In those same verses, Richard Horsley sees the promise that the poor will be delivered from their exploiters. *The Liberation of Christmas*, 68.

29 His work on tribalism, violence, and reconciliation was of particular interest to Lisa and me, as we both worked in regions rife with similar tensions. See Emmanuel Katongole and Jonathan Wilson-Hartgrove, *Mirror to the Church: Resurrecting Faith after Genocide in Rwanda* (Grand Rapids: Zondervan, 2009).

30 For a good introduction to what it means to be an Israeli Messianic Jew, I recommend "An Introduction to Israeli Messianic Jewish Identity," a chapter Lisa Loden wrote for Salim J. Munayer and Lisa Loden, *Through My Enemy's Eyes: Envisioning Reconciliation in Israel-Palestine* (London: Paternoster, 2013), 72–100.

31 Women Wage Peace (https://womenwagepeace.org.il/en/) is an Israeli grassroots movement formed shortly after the Gaza War in 2014. Their aim is to encourage peace in Israel-Palestine, and they are an inclusive group that embraces Israeli and Palestinian women from any faith tradition.

32 Lisa Loden, "Hear the Mother's Cry: 'Bring Down the Peace,'" (unpublished), shared in personal correspondence with the author.

33 Yael Deckelbaum, "Prayer of the Mothers" (unpublished). See official video with song and footage from the March of Hope at

Yael Deckelbaum, "Yael Deckelbaum / Prayer of the Mothers - Official video," YouTube video, 5:20, November 15, 2016, https://www.youtube.com/watch?v=YyFM-pWdqrY.

Chapter 5

1 Luke 2:1–7.
2 Justo González, *Luke* (Louisville, KY: Westminster John Knox, 2010), 33.
3 See Acts 5:37: "After him Judas the Galilean rose up at the time of the census and got people to follow him," triggering an ill-fated rebellion attempt. This was, according to some, the census under Quirinius. Tannehill, *Luke*, 64.
4 Horsley, *The Liberation of Christmas*, 35.
5 Borg and Crossan, *The First Christmas*, 147–49.
6 Borg and Crossan, 150.
7 This sentiment is explained well by Kenneth E. Bailey, *Jesus through Middle Eastern Eyes: Cultural Studies in the Gospels* (Downers Grove, IL: IVP Academic, 2008), 31–34.
8 Phillips Brooks, "O Little Town of Bethlehem," 1868. Public domain.
9 Kelley Nikondeha, "A Modern Innkeeper in Bethlehem," *The Plough*, December 23, 2019, https://www.plough.com/en/topics/culture/holidays/christmas-readings/a-modern-innkeeper-in-bethlehem.
10 It is not uncommon to hear Palestinian Christians refer to themselves as "living stones" in contrast to the ancient limestone buildings across the landscape. They are the stones that continue to testify with their words, lives, and very presence to Jesus in this holy land.

Chapter 6

1 The origin of the town of Bethlehem has been linked to the Canaanites, and so the name to "House of Bread" in their language. But that would have been a distant memory by the time of Bethlehem as we know it. Nicholas Blincoe, *Bethlehem: Biography of a Town* (New York: Nation Books, 2017), 6.
2 Horsley, *The Liberation of Christmas*, 100.
3 Israel-Palestine today continues as a surveillance state. Through high-level technology and low-tech methods like informants, Israel listens and knows what is afoot in the Occupied Territories. In unguarded moments, Palestinians will mention

NOTES

the fact that they are always being watched, with neighbors reporting on you if it shields loved ones from the ire of the state.

4 In Kirundi, the language of Burundi, the literal translation of their morning greeting is "Did you survive the night?" It tells of many generations of nights full of peril when the best greeting was confirmation of survival, literally living to see another day. While the language is different, I imagine the sentiment in ancient Palestine was similar for shepherds and their kin.

5 About the political nature of this title and announcement, see Justo L. González, *Luke*, 35–36.

6 The Tamimi family, featured in chapter 5, lives under a demolition order even now. Demolition orders can be about retaliation for resistance to Israel's occupation or a way to punish those who build without proper permits (which are nearly impossible for Palestinian families to secure from the Israeli government), or merely to clear the land for more settlement construction. The separation wall built for security reasons also serves to separate families from their farmland, and roads that service the settlement population also cut off Palestinian access to their lands, making it immensely difficult to cultivate and tend their ancestral property.

7 For a good introduction to the issues related to land dispossession in the West Bank, I recommend Elie Pritz, "Nassar Family, Israel/Palestine," *Peace Heroes*.

8 Recall the May 2021 protests in the Sheik Jarrah neighborhood over the looming forced evictions of several Palestinian families that resulted in days of violent action involving Gaza, Hamas, and the Israeli war planes. A month later came the actual demolition of one hundred homes in the Silwan neighborhood of Al-Bustan, as well as in East Jerusalem. The action makes way for a "biblical theme park" on the site. (See @sbeih.jpg on Twitter and Instagram.) The anticipated result was the eviction and dispossession of 1,500 Palestinians.

9 The Ottoman Empire lasted from the fourteenth century to 1917. It was followed by British Mandate, 1920–1947.

10 These are not tiny or benign enclaves. The largest settlement, Beitar Illit, has a population of more than 40,000. Sami Tamimi and Tara Wigley, *Falastin: A Cookbook* (New York: Ten Speed Press, 2020), 130–33.

11 Romans 12:17–21.

NOTES

Chapter 7

1 A. Schalit, "The End of the Hasmonean Dynasty and the Rise of Herod" in *The Herodian Period*, ed. Michael Avi-Yonah, vol. 7, *The World History of the Jewish People* (New Brunswick: Rutgers University Press, 1975), 51. Early on, Herod distinguished himself as the first to provide his quota of tribute to Rome. This won him favor with Roman leaders and opened the door for political promotion.

2 Schalit, 44–45. This move helped Herod with Roman relations but put him at odds with the Jewish Sanhedrin, the highest tribunal in the land, which had the power to enact capital punishment. When he took matters of capital punishment into his own hands, he made things worse in terms of his connection with Jewish leaders in Judea.

3 Concerning dynamics that contributed to Herod's insecurity, see M. Stern, "The Reign of Herod," in *The Herodian Period*, 72.

4 Masada's fame is from a subsequent season when Sicarii, Jewish rebels, battled the Romans in another rebellion. They took refuge in the fortress and eventually committed mass suicide rather than be taken by Roman soldiers.

5 Stern, "The Reign of Herod," 75. Herod would have to answer for his part in the assassination of the young high priest, but in the end, Antony seemed to accept his political rationale for the move.

6 For more about the metaphor of adoption, family, and belonging in Scripture, see Kelley Nikondeha, *Adopted: The Sacrament of Belonging in a Fractured World* (Grand Rapids: Eerdmans, 2017).

7 Nicolaus of Damascus reported that Herod's father, Antipater, was descended from Jewish families returned from captivity in Babylon. Josephus wrote that Nicolaus said this to flatter Herod, bending the truth in the process. *Antiquities* 14.15.2, see Avi-Yonah, *The Herodian Period*, 29, and 340n.21.

8 Later in Matthew's Gospel, Jesus will be called King of the Jews, as written in the charge nailed above him on the cross. Matthew 27:37.

9 Luke 4:28–30.

10 Luke 4:16–29; Mark 5:1–20.

11 "Let me offer this as a way the Bible thinks about justice: Justice is to sort out what belongs to whom, and to return it to them." Walter Brueggemann, "Voices of the Night—Against Justice," in Brueggemann, Sharon Parks, and Thomas H. Groome, *To Act Justly, Love Tenderly, Walk Humbly: An Agenda for Ministers* (New York: Paulist, 1986), 4–5.

NOTES

12 For more about the economic elements of divorce Joseph had to consider, refer to Craig S. Keener, *Matthew* (Downers Grove, IL: InterVarsity, 1997), 62–63.

13 Keener, 63–64.

14 Walter Brueggemann preaches powerfully on the first Joseph, his economic practice, and his regrets. See "Taking a Second, Painful Look" in *Threat of Life: Sermons on Pain, Power, and Weakness* (Minneapolis: Fortress, 1996), 9–16, and "A Fourth-Generation Sellout" in *The Collected Sermons of Walter Brueggemann* (Louisville, KY: Westminster John Knox, 2011), 164–67.

15 Warren Carter, *Matthew and the Margins: A Sociopolitical and Religious Reading* (Maryknoll, NY: Orbis, 2000), 66.

16 Isaiah 7:14–16.

17 Isaiah 7:9.

18 The Romans sacked Jerusalem and destroyed the temple in 70 CE. Matthew wrote to his community, likely in Antioch, a decade or so later.

19 Parts of the foregoing text were originally published here: Kelley Nikondeha, "ShePonders: Emmanuel," *SheLoves Magazine*, December 6, 2012, https://shelovesmagazine.com/2012/sheponders-emmanuel/.

20 Matthew 28:20.

21 Luke names Eli as Joseph's father in Luke 3:23 ("Heli" in NRSV). Matthew's use of Jacob points us back to Genesis 37:1–4). Carter, *Matthew and the Margins*, 64.

22 See citation of midrash in Avivah Gottlieb Zornberg, *The Particulars of Rapture: Reflections on Exodus* (New York: Schocken, 2001), 68–70. Also see Kelley Nikondeha, *Defiant: What the Women of Exodus Teach Us about Freedom* (Grand Rapids: Eerdmans, 2020), 80–81.

23 Borg and Crossan, *The First Christmas*, 101.

24 "Economic emancipation" is a term coined by Walter Brueggemann. See Brueggemann, *Texts Under Negotiation: The Bible and Postmodern Imagination* (Minneapolis: Augsburg Fortress, 1993), 76.

Chapter 8

1 Banksy is a London-based street artist. See the image here: "Banksy in Bethlehem! Banksy Street Art, Bethlehem, Palestine," *The Whole World Is a Playground*, February 11, 2021, https://www.thewholeworldisaplayground.com/banksy-bethlehem-street-art/.

NOTES

2 For images, see https://images.app.goo.gl/
   NkuSaAX6oACE6UtQA and https://images.app.goo.gl/
   BYcX3RNQfM5EDYQb7.

3 The Walled Off Hotel was opened in 2017 just across from the
   separation wall with "the worst view of any hotel in the world."
   It is connected to Banksy and a collective of other artists. In
   addition to guest rooms, the site includes a small museum, an art
   gallery featuring Palestinian artists, and the Wall Mart gift shop.
   It is a unique combination of hospitality, business, and social
   commentary.

4 Samuel K. Eddy, *The King Is Dead: Studies in Near Eastern
   Resistance to Hellenism 334–31 B.C.* (Lincoln: University of
   Nebraska Press, 1961; repr. Eugene, OR: Wipf & Stock, 2020).

5 Horsley, *The Liberation of Christmas*, 58.

6 Eddy, *The King Is Dead*, 4–5.

7 Eddy, 3.

8 For an overview of the Persian Empire, see "Persian Empire,"
   History, updated September 30, 2019, https://www.history.com/
   topics/ancient-middle-east/persian-empire. This was also the
   time frame when Cyrus allowed the Jews still in captivity in
   Babylon to return to Jerusalem and rebuild their temple and city,
   as recorded in the book of Ezra.

9 Worship, or *proskynesis*, meant "doing obeisance", or paying
   ceremonial acts of respect to rulers. Horsley, *The Liberation of
   Christmas*, 55. The word also has a political connotation, that of
   prostrating oneself before another. As Carter notes, since the
   magi do not worship Herod, they've made their choice clear.
   Carter, *Matthew and the Margins*, 76.

10 Herod had Aristobulus III killed in around 35 BCE, when the
   popular young high priest threatened to overshadow Herod and
   possibly make a play for his throne.

11 Micah 5:2.

12 The Six-Day War happened in June 1967. Sliman Mansour was
   twenty years old at the time. "Six-Day War," *History*, updated
   August 21, 2018, https://www.history.com/topics/middle-east/
   six-day-war.

13 TRT World, "Sliman Mansour's Work" (video, 7:41),
   Showcase, June 18, 2021, https://www.youtube.com/
   watch?v=CFrOSpLPJNs.

14 This is one account of the interview, as recorded by Faten
   Nastas Mitwasi in his book *Sliman Mansour: An Artist from
   Palestine: Steadfastness and Creativity* (Fulda, Germany: Fuldaer
   Verlagsanstalt, 2008). In a filmed interview, Mansour tells of the
   officer volunteering the idea of the watermelon.

NOTES

15 Mitwasi, 23.

16 Mitwasi, 15.

17 "Palestine: The First Intifada (1987–1993)," *Fanack*, January 31, 2011, https://fanack.com/palestine/history-of-palestine/the-first-intifada/. The Intifada, which lasted from 1987 to 1993, was a grassroots response to the Israeli occupation of the West Bank. One key image showcasing the power disparity is young Palestinians throwing stones at Israeli military tanks.

18 Mansour partnered with Nabil Anani, Tayseer Barakat, and Vera Tamari to form the New Visions Group and engage in shared resistance during the Intifada and beyond.

19 Sliman Mansour, interview by Stefanie Dekker for Al Jazeera, June 26, 2021, https://www.youtube.com/watch?v=SwX5q_y8I6k.

20 See also the poetry of Najwan Darwish, the liberation theology of Naim Ateek and Mitri Raheb, the culinary artistry of Fadi Kattan and Sami Tamini, and the heirloom seed library curated by Vivian Sarsour. Art and resistance come in many forms across the Palestinian landscape and diaspora.

21 Three gifts are listed in Matthew 2:11, which is why the church began to assume there were three magi. But in truth, there could have been two or ten wise men; the narrative does not specify.

Chapter 9

1 Matthew once again hints at the exodus narrative here, and that becomes clearer with his mention (2:15) of Hosea 11:1, which speaks of one called out of Egypt. The quintessential Jewish story of liberation is never far from view as Matthew composes his advent account.

2 Exodus 12:34.

3 "No one leaves home unless home is the mouth of a shark." Warsan Shire, "Home" (oral presentation by the author; video, 3:42), March 13, 2017, https://www.youtube.com/watch?v=nI9D92Xiygo.

4 Those who remain on the land, even amid tumult, are the meek of the world. Mitri Raheb articulates this powerfully in *Faith in the Face of Empire: The Bible through Palestinian Eyes* (Maryknoll, NY: Orbis, 2014), 96–99. He points out, in particular, that the Palestinian people are among the meek who inherit the land.

5 "Israelis sell expired products underground to Palestinian importers." Katrien Hertog, "Library on Wheels for Non-violence and Peace: Study on Best Practices of Active Non-violence," Pax Christi International, Utrecht, 2010, https://fr.nvcwiki.com/images/Pr%C3%A9sentation_LOWNP_en_anglais.pdf, 11.

NOTES

6 Elie Pritz, "Nafez Assaily, Israel-Palestine," *Peace Heroes*. It appears there are still messianic hopes active in Palestine. On a personal note, I am grateful to Elie Pritz for introducing me to Assaily's story.

7 As of 2010, he had reached over 50,000 villagers with books. In the year 2009 alone, he visited eighty-three villages and lent 11,426 books to 1,496 children. Hertog, "Library on Wheels."

8 The campaign was called Books Across the Divide: Reading on the Checkpoints.

9 Hertog, "Library on Wheels," 9.

10 Carter, *Matthew and the Margins*, 84–85.

11 Rachel, beloved wife of Jacob, was mother to some of the twelve sons of Israel.

12 Jeremiah 31:15, quoted in Matthew 2:18; Lamentations 1:1–5. The daughter of Zion is a personification of Jerusalem.

13 Jeremiah 31:17.

14 Walter Brueggemann clarifies that Jeremiah speaks a word of promise, not prediction, in these verses. *A Commentary on Jeremiah: Exile and Homecoming* (Grand Rapids: Eerdmans, 1998), 267.

15 In Jeremiah 40:1 we see that captives from Jerusalem and Judea were in Ramah in preparation for transport to Babylon.

16 Ramah, located on the northern edge of Bethlehem, is not to be confused with Ramallah, a town farther north, in the heart of the West Bank. Rachel's Tomb in Ramah was traditionally honored as a place of remembrance for all three Abrahamic faiths. After the Six-Day War in 1967, Israel annexed the site. Now the only way to enter is under Israeli control, through Israel.

17 Kathleen O'Connor, *Jeremiah: Pain and Promise* (Minneapolis: Fortress, 2012), 110.

18 Jeremiah 31:16 speaks of Rachel's reward for her work, and that work is her unabashed and unrelenting lament.

19 Recall Luke's advent narrative, and how he and his community knew that patience was a part of the advent trajectory too.

Chapter 10

1 Josephus, *Antiquities of the Jews, Book XVII*, 9.3.

2 It is interesting to see that organized mourning as protest drew the ire of the ruler, that mourning has power to disrupt empires and their leaders. The public expression of grief unnerves the imperial apparatus.

3 Justin Butcher, *Walking to Jerusalem: Blisters, Hope and Other Facts on the Ground* (London: Hodder & Stoughton, 2018), 229.

NOTES

4 Walid Khalidi, ed., *All That Remains: The Palestinian Villages Occupied and Depopulated by Israel in 1948* (Washington, DC: Institute for Palestine Studies, 1992). This documents many, though not all, of the villages that suffered forced eviction and destruction in 1948.

5 Butcher, *Walking to Jerusalem*, 229.

6 It has been posited that in reality, Joseph may have migrated north for economic reasons. Horsley, *The Liberation of Christmas*, 71–72.

7 Richard A. Horsley, *Bandits, Prophets, and Messiahs: Popular Movements in the Time of Jesus* (Harrisburg, PA: Trinity Press International, 1985).

8 Only Luke records the account of Joseph, Mary, and Jesus in Jerusalem. Matthew, Mark, and John make no mention of any other incident involving Joseph.

9 Powerfully posited by Borg and Crossan in *The First Christmas*, 76–78.

10 Matthew 5:5.

11 Psalm 37:1–4.

12 Some scholars, like Otto Kaiser, think this psalm was written during the Maccabean period. Walter Brueggemann, *The Psalms: The Life of Faith* (Minneapolis: Fortress, 1995), 244.

13 Raheb, *Faith in the Face of Empire*, 96–100.

14 Raheb, 101.

15 For more about Sami Awad and his organization, Holy Land Trust, visit https://www.holylandtrust.org.

Continuations

1 Mitri Raheb, *Bethlehem Besieged: Stories of Hope in Times of Trouble* (Minneapolis: Fortress, 2004), 157.

FOR FURTHER READING

Nothing More to Lose by Najwan Darwish (poetry)
   New York: New York Review Books, 2000.

Justice and Only Justice: A Palestinian Theology of Liberation by Naim Ateek
   Maryknoll, NY: Orbis, 1989.

Bethlehem Besieged: Stories of Hope in Times of Trouble by Mitri Raheb
   Minneapolis: Fortress, 2004.

Faith in the Face of the Empire: The Bible through Palestinian Eyes by Mitri Raheb
   Maryknoll, NY: Orbis, 2014.

This Is Not a Border: Reportage and Reflections from the Palestinian Festival of Literature, edited by Ahdaf Soueif and Omar Robert Hamilton
   New York: Bloomsbury, 2017.

The Lemon Tree: An Arab, a Jew, and the Heart of the Middle East by Sandy Tolan
   New York: Bloomsbury, 2007.

FOR FURTHER READING

ABOUT THE AUTHOR

Kelley Nikondeha is a liberation theologian, author, and community development practitioner. She's the author of *Adopted: The Sacrament of Belonging in a Fractured World* and *Defiant: What the Women of Exodus Teach Us about Freedom*, as well as a contributor to the award-winning *Jesus-Centered Bible* as well as the *New York Times* bestseller *A Rhythm of Prayer: A Collection of Meditations for Renewal*, edited by Sarah Bessey.

She's a long-time student of Israel-Palestine—its faith traditions, modern politics, food culture, and connection to Christian Scriptures. She's made multiple pilgrimages in recent years to meet peacemakers, deepen friendships and learn the lessons of the land. The richness of the region feeds both her theological and political imagination, with love and lament in turn. It regularly intersects with how she writes about belonging, liberation, and now, Advent.

Kelley serves as the co-director and chief storyteller for Communities of Hope, a community development enterprise in Burundi. She also the co-founder of Amahoro Africa, a ten-year conversation between theologians and practitioners within the African context. She works in Burundi alongside her husband, Claude Nikondeha; he the consummate practitioner and she the resident theologian. Their collaboration allows her to live between Burundi and the US.

A practical theologian at heart, Kelley weaves story and Scripture together to create fresh insight and cultivate faithful practice among faith communities. She loves justice and jubilee wherever she finds it in the world.

ABOUT THE COVER ARTIST

Sliman Mansour

Born in 1947, Mansour spent his childhood around the verdant hills and fields of Birzeit—where he was born—and later his adolescence in Bethlehem and Jerusalem. These experiences left a significant mark on his work, heightening a sense of gradual loss in Palestine, especially after the occupation of the West Bank and Jerusalem in 1967. His early experiences also presented him with the symbols and images he would later use to preserve and highlight Palestinian identity.

ABOUT THE COVER ARTIST

By using symbols derived from Palestinian life, culture, history, and tradition, Mansour uniquely illustrates Palestinians' resolve and connection with their land. His pieces epitomize art as a form of resistance. With the landscape of Palestine and its stone terraces, he represents the mark of Palestinian farmers on the land. With images of Jerusalem, and the glistening Dome of the Rock, he represents the Palestinian homeland and the dream of return.

For the better part of a century, Sliman Mansour's art has deftly reflected the hopes and realities of a people living under occupation. Since the early 1970s, he has translated his experiences of isolation, displacement, community, and rootedness using imagery and symbols that have contributed to the development of an iconography of the Palestinian struggle.

Sliman Mansour is now considered one of the most distinguished and renowned artists in Palestine today. His work—which has come to symbolize the Palestinian national identity—has inspired generations of Palestinians and international artists and activists alike.

For more about Mansour, his career, and artwork, visit www.slimanmansour.com. He also curates an active presence on Instagram at @sliman.mansour.

This abridged profile, an excerpt from the comprehensive biography on Mansour's website as well as the artist's photo, was used with the artist's permission.